Laurie Schaffner

Teenage Runaways
Broken Hearts and "Bad Attitudes"

*Pre-publication
REVIEWS,
COMMENTARIES,
EVALUATIONS . . .*

"***T****eenage Runaways: Broken Hearts and 'Bad Attitudes,'* shows us in vivid terms how we, the parents, helpers, and institutions, are producing generations of 'lost ones.' The youths portrayed in this book, our sons and daughters, are destined to be lost to death, disease, homelessness, and lifelong institutionalization unless we create solutions that match the problems. Schaffner helps us hear the voices and guides us to a compassionate understanding of the struggles facing our systematically disempowered youth. Most important, she then compels the reader to go beyond mere understanding to knowing that we must create solutions that work, save lives, and empower our brokenhearted youth."

Norma Hotaling, BS
*Founder and Director,
SAGE Project,
Exploited Youth Recovery Program
San Francisco, CA*

More pre-publication
REVIEWS, COMMENTARIES, EVALUATIONS . . .

"Laurie Schaffner has skillfully combined the authentic voice of the juvenile runaway with the principles of social science research. She blends the life stories of these runaway youths with a sound structural analysis. This sociological frame demonstrates how the personal reflects the structural context of their family lives and the community. I particularly like the manner in which she combines the sociology of emotions with the concepts of social control theory. The lives and experiences of these youths are seen, in some ways, as a realistic response to the conditions of their own lives. At the same time, she raises questions about their life chances once they leave the assumed protections of family lives.

In focusing on the emotions underlying the act of running away, this book provides an understanding of the complicated—and often contradictory—motivations of runaway youth. The connections among personal motivations and constraints of choice are illustrated in the narratives describing the decision to run away from home. This book is a strong first effort."

Barbara Owen, PhD
Professor,
Department of Criminology,
California State University, Fresno

"Laurie Schaffner provides a compelling examination of teenage runaways, venturing beyond the individual and/or social perspectives often used to describe runaway behavior. Using a social psychological framework, she examines the complex interactions between youths and social institutions, reflecting on their life stories and describing the runaway experience from their viewpoint. Schaffner also introduces emotion theory to explain the social effects of emotion on the behavior of adolescents who run away.

This work deepens our understanding of why youths run away by describing this behavior as a search for attachment and connection—connection to safe and supportive peers, institutions, and communities. It is a must read for academics and practitioners concerned about the alarming rise in teenage runaways and the policy and program responses needed to address this serious social problem."

Barbara Bloom, PhD
Assistant Professor,
Administration of Justice Department,
San Jose State University,
California

"**T**his book is a sensitive and sophisticated look inside the interpretive worlds of teenage runaways. Drawing on in-depth interviews with runaway teens, Laurie Schaffner examines teens' motivations for running away; their quest for meaningful connections with peers, family, and social institutions; and their emotions of sadness, fear, and anger. Her analysis of the emotions associated with running away is particularly insightful. Drawing on the sociology of emotions, Schaffner argues that teenage runaways use their feelings of rage and resentment as a source of power and resistance in the face of what they perceive as unjust treatment by their families and social services. Using the teens' own words, as well as her own insightful descriptions of their demeanor and tone of voice, Schaffner deftly elucidates the multiple layers of emotion that underlie the rupture and reconstruction of runaways' bonds with their families, and the strategies that runaways develop for maintaining a sense of self as they navigate social services.

Schaffner began this project as her undergraduate honors thesis at Smith College. An adult student, her experiences as a young runaway have combined with her impressive analytical skills to produce a work that is both sympathetic to the perspectives of the runaways and provides a fresh theoretical approach. She extends the sociological analysis of emotions in new and creative directions. This book should be read by anyone interested in the perceptions of teenage runaways themselves. Often impressively articulate, the young people Schaffner interviewed shed a fresh light on their dilemmas and on social policy regarding youths and families."

Nancy Whittier, PhD
Assistant Professor,
Smith College,
Northhampton, MA

The Haworth Press, Inc.
New York • London • Oxford

Teenage Runaways
Broken Hearts and "Bad Attitudes"

Teenage Runaways
Broken Hearts
and "Bad Attitudes"

Laurie Schaffner

The Haworth Press
New York • London • Oxford

The Haworth Press, Inc., 10 Alice Street, Binghamton, NY 13904-1580

Cover design by Marylouise E. Doyle.

The Library of Congress has cataloged the hardcover edition of this book as:

Schaffner, Laurie.
    Teenage runaways : broken hearts and "bad attitudes" / Laurie Schaffner.
        p.   cm.
    Includes bibliographical references and index.
    ISBN 0-7890-0550-6 (alk. paper)
    1. Runaway teenagers—United States. I. Title.
HV1431.S36 1999
362.74—DC21   98-46115
                                                                                CIP

ISBN 0-7890-0892-0 (pbk.)

For Jarvis,
ever my heart's desire

CONTENTS

ABOUT THE AUTHOR

Laurie Schaffner grew up in Los Angeles, California, in the 1950s, and lived on her own as a teenager, including living in Mexico during the 1970s. Ms. Schaffner completed her Bachelor's degree as an Ada Comstock Scholar at Smith College in Northampton, Massachusetts in 1995. She is currently a PhD candidate in sociology at the University of California at Berkeley, and she teaches gender studies to incarcerated teenage girls at a northern California juvenile detention facility. Her work has earned awards from the American Sociology Association, the American Society of Criminology, and the Society for Applied Anthropology.

CONTRIBUTORS

David Lee Keiser is a teacher and a poet. He is currently completing a doctorate in urban education at the University of California, Berkeley, and has taught at UC Berkeley, San Francisco State University, and at secondary schools in the Bay Area. Despite its implicit danger, he loves high tide.

Esther Madriz, PhD, is Assistant Professor of Sociology at the University of San Francisco, where she teaches Criminology, Deviance and Social Control, and Violence Against Women. She is the author of *Nothing Bad Happens to Good Girls: Fear of Crime in Women's Lives,* and numerous articles in professional journals.

Valentina Sedeno was born and raised in San Francisco. She is currently a peer liaison for the YWCA and formerly a teen advocate in the domestic violence unit for the San Francisco District Attorney's office. She just returned from a writer's camp in New York. Valentina wants to continue to work with Bay Area young women and men and plans to become a therapist.

Martha Torres-McKay was born in Bahia, Brazil, and raised in San Francisco, California. She is working and studying and likes writing, kids, and family.

Foreword

According to recent statistics, almost 3 million people under age eighteen were arrested in the United States by law enforcement agencies. The FBI estimates that juveniles accounted for 19 percent of all arrests. Of those, almost 200,000 young people were arrested for running away from their homes. The gender distribution of young arrestees indicates that 57 percent are female and 41 percent are male.*

Although one in four juvenile arrests in 1996 involved the arrest of a female, the problems faced by "bad girls" have been largely neglected by the criminological literature, in which adult males and boys have been the predominant focus of inquiry. One of the major justifications for this neglect is that boys are much more likely to be involved in the juvenile justice system than girls. This excuse, however, is no longer valid, for during the last decade, girls' presence in the juvenile justice system has been growing at a much faster rate than boys'.

On the few occasions in which girls have entered the criminological debate, they have been stigmatized and considered "worse than boys," or especially deviant. The mass media, particularly, have fostered these images by presenting to a fearful public the most rare and extreme cases of girls' deviance as if they were commonplace occurrences.

In this context, Laurie Schaffner's book is an important contribution to the field of juvenile delinquency. Indeed, her research arrives to fill an existing gap in the literature by presenting the problems faced by runaway boys and girls in a sensitive, compassionate, yet realistic manner. The author's descriptions of the lives of these children are a moving reminder of what many of them face in today's society.

---

*U.S. Department of Justice (1997). Juvenile arrests 1996. *Juvenile Justice Bulletin.* Washington, DC: Office of Juvenile Justice and Delinquency Prevention.

For many years, individualistic explanations of deviance have dominated the field of criminology and juvenile delinquency. In the case of girls, those who do not follow the rules of behavior expected from them in a gendered society are viewed as sick, emotionally unstable, or social misfits. On the contrary, in *Teenage Runaways*, the author avoids simplistic explanations to the problem of children who flee from emotional, psychological, and even sexual trauma. Drawing from interactionist and conflict theories, Schaffner builds a complex framework that allows the reader to comprehend the issue of runaway teenagers in its full social and political dimensions.

Especially important in her analysis is the use of a new area in sociology—emotion theory—in understanding the role of feelings that arise in the lives of runaways. By highlighting the role of emotions, the author emphasizes the point that so-called "bad attitudes" of teenagers, contextualized in the emotional turmoil they face, are in fact expressions of emotions that are derived politically and socially—not solely individually.

Very few books present to the reader in such an intense and vivid manner the anguish and despair that runaways face when dealing with the rupture of family bonds. As the author reminds us, some breaks become irreparable, leaving some young people with few options other than running away from their families and their homes. In fact, the author informs us that most runaways do not want to leave their homes.

Schaffner's interviews with twenty-four teenagers give validity to their voices. She opens new possibilities of research by dealing with an issue that, lamentably, has been ignored in the field of juvenile delinquency: the fear of victimization that many young people experience at the hands of those who are supposed to guard, love, and protect them. Moreover, the Puerto Rican and African-American teenagers included in her sample add value to the book, since most studies in the field largely ignore these groups. As Schaffner reminds us, young people occupy a subordinate position in our society. Children of color face a double marginality that may influence the runaway experience. For example, they may be more likely to be apprehended by law enforcement agencies, or some may be sons and daughters of immigrant parents and face problems of adaptation to a new culture.

Hopefully, sociologists and criminologists will follow the lead set by Laurie Schaffner's research, contributing to obliterate the stereotypical notions that surround us regarding adolescent runaways. Those notions foster images of these children, in general, and of girls, in particular, as "bad" and "difficult" creatures. *Teenage Runaways* stands out as an important contribution that gives a vivid and humane face to the problems encountered by young people in the contemporary United States.

Esther Madriz
University of San Francisco
San Francisco, CA

Preface

I ran away from home in 1969—I was fifteen years old. I did everything in the streets that young girls do to survive, and everything that happens to young girls in the streets happened to me. Why would I begin a scholarly book with a confession such as this? In some circles, it might legitimize the theoretical claims I will make and lend weight to my academic insights. In others, it might undermine my "voice of authority." You will have to decide what you think of the use academia makes of the confessions and biographies of its scholars.

When I was out on the streets, it was a different world. Many of the activities we engaged in then are the same for the youths I meet today: sex, drugs, scams, searching for protection and a way to escape trouble. Yet the 1970s' economy afforded greater opportunity to live on the fringes. We could rent inexpensive apartments, a sack of potatoes was only a few cents, and it was hip to live on the margins of society. Everybody wasn't "homeless," just a freak crowd of hippies who hitchhiked around and camped out. We were not surrounded by an ominous culture of violence or threatened by government reductions of our food stamps and GSS payments. Progressive social movements were vibrant in the 1960s and 1970s, and they supported young people, feelings and love, and change. We had a place to channel our broken hearts and "bad attitudes"—into feminism, anticolonialism, antiracist civil rights actions, labor activist work.

Today, street youths—runaways, kids in trouble—witness adults suffering from "road rage," cutting one another off in their sport utility vehicles. We are all told that the economy is booming, yet most of us have never felt worse. Life may be good, but for someone else, somewhere else. Everyone is busier than ever, and getting ahead never seemed more hopeless. If young people do make it to college, they do so without a sense of social history or the know-how to be critical thinkers. They seem flattened by television and Ritalin.

I quit school in the seventh grade. Years later, when I was thirty-four years old, I was working in a television station as a broadcast engineer. One of my tasks was to screen and evaluate rough footage that the producers brought in from the field. I worked on one documentary about teenage prostitutes—kids who lived on the streets. I was overwhelmed by the images and memories of the street and realized that I had not really revisited much of my youthful trauma and experiences in any meaningful way. Mostly, I had continued on a somewhat seamless trajectory of personal and emotional confusion, trouble, and strife. I couldn't believe all that misery was still going on; somehow, I guess, I imagined that since I wasn't part of the street life economy anymore, that it must have gotten better for everybody else as well. I began to volunteer and then find work in shelters and group homes and saw firsthand how suffering had persisted for thrown-away, abused youths. I decided to go back to school to "figure out what was going on." This study is my first attempt at that project—the project to integrate my life story, my learned wisdom with my new life as a scholar, my history of commitment to community activism, and my care for my social world.

Remember two things about this book. One, it attempts to follow in the footsteps of others who bring the voices of the "subjects" themselves to the fore of theorizing. Can the subaltern speak? "Hell, yeah!" as the youths say. Empirically anchored work makes way for their voices to lead the discussion. Second, the theoretical arguments are an attempt to synthesize structural *and* emotional explanations of troubles. Poverty, patriarchy, and racism spawn righteous anger and despair. These institutional and emotional experiences are simultaneously intertwined, reflexive, causative, and liberatory. Emotional experience, paradoxically, can lead to oppression—is the resultant effect of oppression—and can lead to ways out.

So, what can be done for teenage runaways? We need to listen to them, and to all troubled youths, very carefully. They tell us the answers all the time in their lyrics and poetry and life stories (see their recommendations in Chapter 5). They know that they need us—to listen to them, trust them, believe in them, inspire them. They need us to give them better attention, love, care, and to provide them with a good education and employment. Maybe we do not need to reinvent the wheel in our political, cultural, and social systems of care, but we do need to reinvigorate our collaborations and collective efforts to speak out on behalf of young people in the United States. That one in four children live in poverty is the real crime in our society. The overfunded "juvenile correctional" departments inherit all the failings of the underfunded educational, community, and family networks in which young people live and grow. We must unite our efforts—academics, activists, and artists—young and old, and fight these trends toward punitive incarceration and away from education and community cultures of care.

These very youths in trouble eloquently give us the solutions, and I'll let them have the last word, here in this preface and in this book. Thirty years ago, those labeled "youths in struggle" touted slogans such as "Black Is Beautiful," "The Personal Is Political," "Question Authority," and "By Any Means Necessary." Today they are labeled "youths in trouble," yet their slogans remain equally inspiring: "Do the Right Thing," "Rage Against the Machine," "Don't Believe the Hype," and "You Go, Girl!"

Laurie Schaffner

Acknowledgments

Although they must remain anonymous, I would like to thank all the youths—*los jóvenes*—for their generous honesty. You know who you are, in more ways than one. Special thanks to the "adult runaways." Thanks also to everyone at the shelter—the staff and director—for your professional savvy and your sweet, kindhearted openness with me. My colleagues and advisors at Smith College were numerous. Tiertza-Leah Schwartz, Director of SOS, thank you for helping me locate the shelter and encouraging scholar activism. Gretchen Ullrich, thanks for tireless transcriptions, great theory, and great gossip. Special appreciation goes out to researcher extraordinaire Seka Berger at Neilson Library. I have a special place in my heart for Mickey Glazer and Rick Fantasia for gently guiding my methodological and theoretical development. Nancy Whittier, my undergraduate honor's thesis advisor, carefully helped me to say what I wanted to say. Thank you so much for sharing your brilliance, encouragement, wit, and patience and for making this project, and Smith, such a transformative experience.

The honor's thesis "Deviance, Emotion, and Rebellion: The Sociology of Teenaged Runaways" received an honorable mention award from the Peter K. New Prize of the Society for Applied Anthropology in 1995. A version of Chapter 4 received an honorable mention from the Section on the Sociology of Emotion, American Sociology Association, 1995. These "nods" came at tender times in my education, and I hope that professors and readers realize how much this kind of appreciation and recognition means to the beginning scholar.

Other colleagues, friends, and family read and commented on drafts over the years, both during and since Smith: Elizabeth Bernstein, Melinda Blau, Margaret Fiedler, Arlie Hochschild, Lora Box Lempert, and David Matza. All gratitude goes out to them, and all blame for not heeding their advice lies with me. Partial funding was provided by the Abigail Reynolds Hodgen Publication Fund.

God bless everyone who reads this book
and—
do the right thing!

Carlos, fifteen-year-old
awaiting sentencing on auto theft
and runaway charges

Catch Me

Catch me.
I tried to run.
I tried to fly.
My life wasn't kickin it.
I had to say bye.
No longer my mama's baby
Soon to be my baby's mama.

Didn't know what to say.
So I was up
out
off
alone
not grown
but grown.

No one to talk to.
My mami's already stressed.
My girls have their own problems,
Besides . . .
They wouldn't understand.
My man is no longer my man since he realized he had to be a man.

So me and my little one, we travel.
So little and so innocent I don't want her to come into this world
with mama being a lost girl.
But it's too late to show him another.
I have to face the fact
I'm about to be a
mother.

Alone
without a man
or a plan
and damn,
nobody understands.

Martha Torres-McKay

Chapter 1

Running Away Is Social Behavior: Statistics and History

Like there's been times where I've gone to my friends' houses with tears running down, you know, I can't breathe and I'm all upset and everything, and a lot of them went through the same thing. They had Department of Social Service involved in their lives. I never even had that. Their problems are worse then my problems—a lot of my friends were sexually abused or had drug problems or abusive families—but my problems are problems to me. They may not seem big and stuff, but it's my life . . . [Awaiting disposition on an unarmed robbery charge and treatment for a suicide attempt.][1]

Stacey, age sixteen

INTRODUCTION: PROBLEMS IN IDENTIFYING RUNAWAY BEHAVIORS

Far back from a busy county road at the end of a long driveway sits a rambling yellow wooden house and garage. This adolescent shelter had no fences surrounding it, no bars on the windows—runaways would note triumphantly that they could "just walk away from here" if they wanted to. Except for the many cars often parked in the small paved area at the end of the drive, the shelter resembled a ranch-style single-family home. County and state vehicles regularly drove in and out, dropping off shackled charges or picking up young offenders from the two-story residential facility to take them to locked facilities. This was where I spent the 1993-1994 academic year, hanging out, interviewing, and observing teenage runaways to gain a firsthand understanding of the disturbing adolescent behavior of running away from home.

A tragic portion of the next generation consists of a population of young people who are being raised without parents, in shelters, public group houses, and foster care settings. America's children are running away from their homes at a rate of approximately 1 to 1.5 million adolescents a year (National Runaway Switchboard, 1993). That figure represents approximately 2 percent of all adolescents in the nation (Burgess, 1986, p. 3). This rate has remained relatively steady since 1975, and there is no indication of a decline in the trend. Three percent of American families will produce a runaway child in a given year; approximately one in eight American adolescents have run away at least once before the age of eighteen (Burgess, 1986, p. 3; Garbarino, Schellenbach, and Sebes, 1986).

Runaways are defined as youths under the age of eighteen who absent themselves from home or place of legal residence at least overnight without permission of parents or legal guardians (United States General Accounting Office [USGAO], 1989; National Network of Runaway and Youth Services, 1991). A 1990 U.S. Department of Justice report includes a further distinction in its definition: two nights outside of the home for youths over fifteen years of age (Finkelhor, Hotaling, and Sedlak, 1990). Legally, running away is considered a "status offense": it is a crime by virtue of age stratification. In other words, status violations are problems only for those who have not achieved the status of adulthood. Late-night hours (curfew violation), alcohol consumption, sexual activity, truancy, and running away are examples of punishable crimes for minors solely because the offender is under a certain age (sixteen to twenty-one years old, depending on state and local statutes).

Runaway experiences can be grouped in terms of duration of time spent outside the home (Jones, 1988). Some children may leave home for twenty-four hours; others may never return. Long-term runaways' stays outside of the home can be measured in months or years and represent young people whose family ties may have been severed beyond repair (Jones, 1988, p. 25). These youths may be homeless or may have been abandoned. Homeless runaways are a relatively small percentage—reports vary, from 2 percent (USGAO, 1989, p. 20) to 11 percent (Bass, 1992, p. xiii). Other runaways leave home for shorter amounts of time, staying away for only a few hours, indicating that strong connections with their families do exist (Jones, 1988). In a 1990 report, half of the runaways studied returned home within two days (Finkelhor, Hotaling, and Sedlak, 1990, p. 11). However, runaways with long-term chronic family problems are also thought to make up a large percentage of youths—between 27 percent and 38 percent had been in foster care the previous year (1990) (National Association of Social Workers [NASW], 1993). These runaways leave for a few days to a few weeks; some estimate that this is the largest group of runaways (Jones, 1988, p. 24).

Runaway behavior is not only determined by length of stay away from home but also by how the departure is accomplished. In my sample, runaways reported leaving amid emotional and physical fighting, and also through careful calculations of timing and duration of their stays outside the families, group homes, and foster homes they left. Most often, runaways ran to a friend's or neighbor's house, but they also described running to police stations and to phone booths where they called social workers or relatives. Two-thirds of the runaways in a 1990 report ran to a friend's or relative's home (Finkelhor, Hotaling, and Sedlak, 1990, p. 11). Runaways may be escaping long-term family conflict where sexual and physical abuse is reported, or they may leave on impulse, protesting a family quarrel over a rule or an isolated incident.

Most runaways do not run far from home; in my sample, 88 percent of the participants ran fewer than 100 miles away from home. A recent study of runaways found that nine in ten had gone fewer than 100 miles (Finkelhor, Hotaling, and Sedlak 1990, p. 11). Most of the youths in my study were from the rural regions in western Massachusetts, near the shelter, or from nearby states. All of the youths in my sample were in contact with their parents, their foster care guardian, or their social worker at some point during their absence.

A 1989 report on runaways and homeless youths estimated their numbers to be between 1.2 million and 1.5 million each year (Bass, 1992, p. ix).[2] In a 1995 report, approximately 2.8 million youths in the United States reported some type of runaway experience (U.S. Department of Health and Human Services, 1995). Although these total numbers are high, they are believed to be an underestimation. Many runaways are not even counted. Because of the recent development of homelessness in America, and also the emergence of thrown-away and abandoned children, studying and counting runaways is problematic.[3]

Attempts are made to reunite runaways who are apprehended by police or social service agents with their families of origin. However, reunification is possible in only about 50 percent of the cases (NASW, 1993, p. 5). Runaways are then marginalized into a social service network of adolescent shelters, foster families, group homes, and juvenile facilities until their eighteenth birthdays (NASW, 1993, p. 3). If they are never detected as runaways, they become discounted and invisible as homeless youths, usually surviving on the street economy of drug trade, prostitution, and theft (National Network of Runaway and Youth Services, 1994).

Why do teenagers run away from home? How do they feel about it? What are the usual explanations for this behavior? Runaway behaviors include a wide variety of complex activities, and I will continue to elaborate a picture of runaway behavior throughout this book. In this chapter, I will present an overview of the approaches to understanding this problem and introduce ideas that led to this study.

A SOCIAL HISTORY OF RUNNING AWAY

The reasons children cite for fleeing their homes have shifted over time. A history of social attitudes of runaway behavior in America traces the changing perspectives held toward runaways.[4] During the colonial period, striking out for adventure, fame, and fortune was somewhat sanctioned. The United States was becoming a new country, expanding its frontiers and conquering a continent. Davy Crockett and Benjamin Franklin both began their adult lives by running away from their homes. Likewise, trudging the countryside was a common occurrence for young male citizens in search of employment during the early part of this century and the era of the Great Depression. Fictional and popular figures such as Tom Sawyer, Huckleberry Finn, and Horatio Alger embodied the American image of the adventurous maverick—the hero runaway—in American literature and media. In the 1950s, the runaway experience came to be criminalized; runaways began to be characterized as juvenile delinquents. During the 1960s, the term flower children was used to describe youths who eschewed middle-class dominant norms and conventional suburban lifestyles. But the public became alarmed in the 1970s due to an increasing trend toward crime, drug abuse, and prostitution, particularly among America's youths in urban areas.[5] Furthermore, the reporting of sexual and physical abuse in the family rose dramatically in the 1980s. Today, physical and sexual abuse—rather than seeking adventure, work, or criminal activity—is the reason that 50 to 70 percent of adolescents cite for fleeing the family home (U.S. Department of Justice, 1989, p. 1; NASW, 1993, p. 1). The problems and risks for contemporary runaways evolve as much from aberrant behavior within the family as from influences on the streets. Social attitudes are again shifting, and runaways are beginning to be viewed more as victims of abuse rather than juvenile delinquents (Janus et al., 1987, p. 13).

REASONS FOR RUNNING AWAY: POPULAR ASSUMPTIONS, MYTHS, AND CURRENT REALITIES

The nature and severity of the reasons that adolescents cite for running away vary in range from youths who complain about "having to be home on time" (Palenski and Launer, 1987, p. 351) to youths who are being severely beaten and repeatedly sexually abused (Powers and Jaklitsch, 1989, p. 4). Can any one theory or approach encompass these multiple and complex causes? I will present the discussion of the reasons that runaway children offer for fleeing the family to expose three common assumptions regarding the source of the runaway problem. The first assumption explains the cause of running away by "blaming the bad child." The second approach seeks to place the source of the problem with the "bad family" or other institutions, such as an insufficient educational system, social service community, or legal apparatus. The third approach—the one from which this project stems—seeks the source of the runaway problem in the interactions between individuals and the norms and expectations of the culture and institutions that make up our social structures.[6]

Individual Solutions to an Individual Problem

One typical assumption about runaways is that they are "problem children": they have an individual behavioral pathology that an isolated unlucky family has to solve. A common label for runaways has been to consider them delinquent or "bad."

Juvenile delinquency is defined legally as "a form of antisocial behavior . . . typically applied to criminal behaviors of those who are under 16 to 18 years of age," depending on local statutes (Dusek, 1991, p. 371). Delinquency is a term that evolved originally to protect youth offenders from being labeled criminal and prosecuted as adults (Dusek, 1991, p. 371). Delinquent acts include crimes for which adults are also prosecuted, but also status offenses such as running away from home. Running away from home, while considered legally and socially delinquent, is, for many youths from families in conflict, viewed by them as their best option. In one government document, 41 percent of the adolescents report what they perceive as unsolvable problems and emotional conflict in their families that forced them to run away (USGAO, 1989).[7]

Besides placing the sole cause of runaway behavior in a criminal and legal framework, another way to view the runaway as having an individual problem is advanced by using a medical model. This psychiatric framework for evaluating runaway behavior was first suggested in 1971 and is called the "runaway reaction" (Jenkins, 1971, pp. 1032-1039). The American Psychiatric Association (1968) included it as a diagnostic category in the *Diagnostic and Statistical Manual for Mental Disorders,* Second Edition.[8]

The individual pathology perspective of the runaway problem places the cause in the individual (Brennan, Huizinga, and Elliot, 1978, p. 52). This approach highlights "depression, low self-esteem, loneliness, lack of internal impulse control, delinquent tendencies, and subsequent delinquent activities" in individual youths (Janus et al., 1987, p. 49). The runaway is considered "delinquent and pathological," and individual treatment in the form of counseling is recommended (Janus et al., 1987, p. 49).

By dismissing runaway behavior as delinquent, or runaways as solely in need of psychological attention, we miss central issues that speak to the vulnerability of young people in nonfunctioning families.[9] We paint runaways as "tough" or "rotten" and discount their own accounts of running in terror for their lives. We also miss key patterns in runaway behavior that cross individual divisions: runaways share many responses in similar and important ways as groups of troubled adolescents, not as isolated incidents of individual mental or criminal pathology. At any rate, how can the problem of running away be a separate, individual, personal problem for each one of these 1 to 2 million children? Should each runaway be incarcerated in juvenile halls across America and each one given individual psychotherapeutic treatment? And even so, how would individual counseling prevent a runaway from feeling that the best alternative would be to bolt? Sociology, unlike some criminology or psychiatry theories, places runaway behavior in a *social* perspective and considers running away a social problem with social solutions.

Society's Falling Apart: "Blame" Institutions

The approach to the runaway problem that locates the source of the behavior as a family problem is included in an argument that looks at the wider social environment and holds that many of the social structures in the dominant culture are failing. If it isn't the family, then it must be the sinking educational infrastructure, the inefficient legal establishment and social service sector, or lack of youth resources in the municipal community.[10] At any rate, many common beliefs about the development of the runaway problem fall within this assumption that it is a given individual "problem family" or that families are falling apart. Studies discuss the findings that poor and broken families cannot control, or do not respect, their children (Luker, 1991; Janus et al., 1987, pp. 40-42). Others see the rampant abuse in American families as causing the problem (Burgess, 1986; Powers and Jaklitsch, 1989; Kurtz, Kurtz, and Jarvis, 1991; McEvoy and Erickson, 1990). Runaways continually cite irreconcilable differences with their parents as a reason that they flee. Causes of running away, such as "family disturbance, poor communication, and parent-child conflict," are listed in several studies (Rothman, 1991, p. 33). Parents, adult relatives, and family friends are drinking and taking drugs in the house every night. Alcohol and drug abuse problems in the family were cited by 16 percent of runaway youths in one study (USGAO, 1989, p. 24). For 8 percent of runaways in that study, domestic violence was listed as the reason that the children ran away (USGAO, 1989, p. 24). Being pushed out of the house and getting thrown out of school is another reason adolescents leave home and do not return (Brennan, 1980, p. 201; Wilkinson, 1987). Twenty-nine percent of the runaways from the USGAO report list "over-restrictive parents," and on the other side of the spectrum, 18 percent list "parental neglect" as the reason they fled the family home (USGAO, 1989, p. 24).

Physical and Sexual Child Abuse in the Family

Sadly, a discussion of contemporary runaway behavior would be incomplete without considering sexual incest and physical abuse. Choosing a definition of abuse itself has complex implications and influences identification of the behavior: narrow definitions exclude some forms of abuse, and broad definitions include many behaviors that may be inappropriate, but not abusive. Since physical and sexual abuse are reported by so many contemporary runaways, and so many in this study, I will provide the following definitions of abuse, maltreatment, and neglect from Powers and Jaklitsch (1989):

> Physical abuse is considered to have occurred when the adolescent has been nonaccidentally physically harmed in some way, or placed at risk of being physically harmed. (p. 11)

> Neglect. When children of any age are not adequately housed, clothed, or fed, they are being neglected. "Pushouts" or "Throwaways" . . . are young people who do not willingly choose to leave home but are forced to leave by their parents with the intention that they do not return. (p. 12)

> Emotional maltreatment is usually defined in terms of parental behavior that has a demonstrated negative effect on a child's emotional or psychological development and well-being. This may consist of repeated threats of harm, a persistent lack of concern for a child's welfare, bizarre disciplinary measures, or continual demeaning or degrading of a child. (p. 12)

Sexual abuse refers to any sexual offense committed, or allowed to be committed, against a young person by a parent or other person legally responsible for him or her. This may include touching a young person for the purpose of sexual gratification or forcing a young person to touch an adult; sexual intercourse; exposing a young person to sexual activity, exhibitionism, or pornography; or permitting a young person to engage in sexual activity that is not developmentally appropriate. (p. 13)

Escaping physical and sexual abuse is such a frequent reason for fleeing the family (Wilkinson, 1987; Roberts, 1982; Adams, Gullotta, and Clancy, 1985) that a recent national update on runaway and homeless shelter residents reported that "between 60 percent and 70 percent of youths in shelters and transitional living facilities nationwide were physically or sexually abused by parents" (NASW, 1993, p. 1). Young people are increasingly reporting physical or sexual abuse inside the family: the estimated number of child abuse victims jumped 40 percent between 1985 and 1991 (Adler, 1994). Assessing the accuracy of self-reported incidents of child abuse is a complex and highly charged social issue. Licensed social workers, police agents, teachers, and school psychologists furnish statistics that appear to corroborate the evidence reported by thousands of youths (Janus et al., 1987, pp. 9-11; Powers and Jaklitsch, 1989, p. 4). Adolescent runaways who flee this sexual and physical abuse are desperate. As one study of runaways reports:

When the chronicity of running results from abusive treatment in the home, it signals that the child or adolescent does not have any other strategy for coping with or avoiding the abuse except to flee to the streets, to friends, or to another adult's protection. (Janus et al., 1987, p. 36)

Working to identify, understand, and heal child abuse has become a social service industry and academic discipline of its own, replete with the development of literature, theory, and treatment practice.

Special problems develop in the treatment of runaways who have run from physical and sexual abuse because the maltreatment of runaways is frequently not recognized, reported, or treated (Powers and Jaklitsch, 1989, p. 5). The children are picked up by the police for crime, drugs, prostitution, homelessness, or a status offense such as truancy, or they are seen in emergency rooms in hospitals across the nation. However, the root cause of the criminal behavior or medical condition is often some form of undiscovered maltreatment in the family at home (Powers and Jaklitsch, 1989, p. 5).

Scholars note that it is imperative not to underestimate the psychological, emotional, and behavioral effects that incestuous rape and physical beatings within the family have on runaways (Powers and Jaklitsch, 1989, p. 11). Growing up and leaving home is difficult for a "normal" family to manage and for teenagers to survive intact (Steinberg, 1990, p. 265; Powers and Jaklitsch, 1989, p. 21). But, homeless and runaway youths who have experienced incest or been physically assaulted face special separation problems. They have not resolved the issues with their parents, so they repeatedly reexperience the stress of earlier losses in many of their post-runaway situations (Powers and Jaklitsch, 1989, p. 21).

The viewpoint of "blaming" runaway behavior on social structures and environmental factors such as the family dynamics of abusive parental behavior leads "advocates of this position [to] believe that it is reasonable to expect youths to try to escape from these environments" (Janus et al., 1987, p. 49). Sexual assault, incest, and physical abuse within families often initiates social worker or legal intervention into the family, and social complications arise at that juncture. An American norm regarding privacy in the family is reflected in historical and widespread resistance to governmental meddling and intervention in the personal lives of Americans. The family is held as almost a sacrosanct American institution, and, therefore, it is difficult to ascertain exactly what is going on behind the front door of "a man's castle." As Janus and colleagues note, disclosure is incomplete and "because our culture believes in the sanctity of the family and the family's right to privacy, some endemic familial abuse is missed" (1987, p. 116). At any rate, although incest and physical abuse are salient features of the contemporary runaway problem, they are not the only problems in American families today that influence runaway behavior.

An understanding of runaway conditions requires a careful evaluation of family issues. Further probes reveal that not all young abuse victims run away, and not all child victims of abuse cite abuse as their primary reason for running away. Therefore, abuse—in its broadest term—is a necessary, but not sufficient, factor in runaway behavior. Other factors must be involved. Another common myth about runaways is that they come from poor families that are socioeconomically deprived.

The Culture of Poverty: Runaways Come from "Under-Class" Families

Another tempting argument in faulting social institutions for the runaway problem would be to adopt the common misconception that children from poor families run away more often, that the tensions in working-class families are somehow emotionally and psychologically worse than the problems of middle-class families, or that working poor people cannot control their children. Although it is true that particular social classes influence family problems differently (Rubin, 1976, pp. 7-8), teenagers are responding to a crisis in American families—no matter the economic situation at home. Actually, one national report found that less than 10 percent of homeless or runaway youths come from families on public assistance and only 11 percent of homeless youths came from families in which unemployment was a problem (USGAO, 1989). A 1988 New York study found that 21 percent of the youths seeking social services came from households that received public assistance (USGAO, 1989).

A 1993 study of runaways using homeless and runaway shelters nationwide notes that 48 percent of the youths receiving assistance are from families with long-term economic problems (NASW, 1993, p. 2). In another report, the breakdown of runaways by socioeconomic background of their parents revealed that 39 percent of families lived below the national poverty line, 34 percent were working class, 21 percent were middle class, and 6 percent were upper middle class (National Network of Runaway and Youth Services, 1991, p. 6). These researchers found that reports of the "increase in youth from poor and working-class families over the past decade appear to correspond with the overall economic status changes in the U.S. population" (National Network of Runaway and Youth Services, 1991, p. 6). Although it is not my intention to deemphasize the key role that socioeconomic status plays in the lives of the families of runaways, it is important to note that the cause of this behavior cannot be neatly laid at the feet of "poverty" or "under-class" behavior.

A careful look at the previously cited 1993 NASW data indicates that 52 percent of the clients in that study are *not* from families with long-term economic problems. Brennan and colleagues note that in one study, for families with annual incomes under $7,000, the runaway rates were higher (by 4.2 percent) than for families with higher incomes. However, they did find that there were "no differences in runaway rates according to whether the chief wage earner in the family was in a white-collar or blue-collar job" (Brennan, Huizinga, and Elliott, 1978, p. 5). Although these data do debunk the myth that the teenage crisis of running away occurs more often in working-class and poor families, the experience of poverty, disadvantage, and need will influence the New York City street survivor differently from a Palm Beach teen crashing at a friend's pad.[11] It is crucial to emphasize that the socioeconomic status of the parents of runaways has a key influence on runaway behavior, particularly on the alternatives and resources that runaways have at their disposal, but it is inaccurate to say that most runaways come from extremely poor backgrounds.

Considering the widespread assumption that the family structure—with problems of abuse and money worries in particular—is the source of the runaway problem, raises the following question: Should each individual family have its own social service worker assigned to patrol it to ensure that no incest or physical abuse occurs? We know that running away is not simply a low-income problem because we see that runaways also run from middle-class homes in which the chief wage earners have professional jobs. If runaway behavior is not always individual, and it is not purely structural, what other approaches will help form a cohesive analysis of the patterns of runaway behavior? My research began to move away from the popular "blame the individual" and "blame the family" approaches, to listening more carefully to what the runaways were reporting.[12]

DEVELOPMENT OF RUNAWAY CULTURE THROUGH PATTERNS OF EMOTIONAL INTERACTION

A third approach to understanding runaway behavior utilizes ideas from both individual and social environment perspectives, but focuses on the relationships between individuals and the social structures. This is done by examining the complex interactions between youths and the immediate social institutions in which they circulate—in families (especially in their relations with parents), among friends, at school, and in community structures. This interactionist approach places runaway phenomena into a social-psychological framework—not exclusively psychiatric, as in the first approach, nor completely social, as in the second. Brennan, Huizinga, and Elliott describe the interactionist approach to understanding runaway behavior as placing the cause as "inhering in the joint interaction between the person and the environment," which allows for acknowledging a "variety of different kinds of runaways from a variety of different kinds of social conditions" (1978, p. 43).

The interactionist approach to the study of runaway behavior focuses on the accounts of the youths as they interact in the cultural norms of structures and institutions of which their environments consist. It examines the ways that they attempt to make sense of these interactions. Symbolic interactionism is sometimes considered a "sociology of everyday life."

Interaction does not take place in a vacuum, nor in pristine settings of isolated individuals and families. Humans gather in society, and society is stratified inequitably. I found that recognizing a perspective of conflict inherent in the runaways' subordinate position in the family added to a more complete understanding of runaway behavior. Conflict perspective posits that interactions are based on struggles over material and symbolic resources. Through the use of symbolic interaction and conflict perspective, a deeper analysis develops that explains why some children run away and others don't. This analysis also provides notions about how runaway rates might be minimized, and amelioration in the lives of individual runaways begun. Using these perspectives to analyze runaway behavior might include listening to stories about running away in order to understand this problem.

EMOTION THEORY AND RUNNING AWAY

Although the various types of reasons behind the decision to run away are key elements in understanding adolescent runaway behaviors, this book considers another related dimension in the lives of teens. Using interaction and conflict perspective, this study examines the social meaning of how runaways feel about events in their lives—the families they left and their lives on the run—and how these emotions affect their interpretations of their experiences. Using a new area in sociology, the sociology of emotion, this research questions how runaway teenagers make sense of events in their family situations—in the homes they have left, in the places they have run to—and how they feel about being runaways, about being sifted through the social service system. I am interested in the role of emotion in their lives: how they "use" their feelings, how they define and describe the origin of their emotions, and how and where the runaways direct their emotions. I will argue that the "bad attitudes" and emotional lives of adolescents on the run is a political and social phenomenon, that through understanding the social implications of their emotions, we can better understand how to help these troubled youths.

Since this study looks at the influence of emotion in runaways' decisions to run, examining the accounts that runaways provide will be central. The stories that youths render will contain descriptions of their perspectives and their perceptions about the events in their lives. Ascertaining whether these accounts are "true" is not the mission of this book. Indeed, it is exactly the runaways' perceptions that are key—because from their experience of the events in their lives come the emotions that guide runaway behaviors.

How youths describe their lives and feelings reveals the quality of emotions that animate their perspectives. Through interviews and participation/observation at a local shelter, I gathered the life stories of twenty-four young people. I examined the social forces surrounding their feelings about running away and about surviving life on the run. I will present this data and show that, from the runaways' perspectives, youths ran from heartbreaking and violent scenes and from drunken, oblivious parents to friends' houses and social hangouts. Their accounts revealed that some runaways struggled to remain in school, attending their classes from the houses of wherever they were crashing. They stayed in groups, hanging out together, making decisions through their gossiping, nurturing, and socializing with one another, partying and drinking in groups, and using and selling drugs to one another—trying to survive together.

I will show that runaway behavior is emotional behavior. One after another, these adolescents related horror stories of brutal, angry, physical fights with family members in fits of rage. Fear, rage, disbelief, hurt—an insane emotional chaos—was described repeatedly. Other factors, such as drug and alcohol abuse, location of and connection with peers, and confronting violence and sexual assault, were each considered in moments of emotional decision making by these distraught and fed-up young people.

Some of their decisions to run away were strategic and political. To escape a frightening and unhealthy environment, such as a home in which there is repeated incest, children have to summon a huge reserve of strength. I will show how their feelings became battlegrounds of struggle and growth—as they agonized over the need to absolve their parents, yet protect themselves. They were quick to excuse their parents or qualify their departures with statements such as, "I love my mother. I would never hurt her, but . . . " As youth after youth related his or her tale, I pondered the social and emotional processes that some youths had to go through to survive some of the worst experiences in American family life.

I will show that emotion theory, combined with conflict and interaction perspectives, provides the seeds of a comprehensive and cohesive new understanding of runaway behavior. I became convinced that a sociological perspective on emotion is missing from the deviance and juvenile delinquency literature and that interaction and conflict perspectives, combined with understanding the role of emotion, would help to illuminate the emotional underpinnings of runaway behaviors. Emotion theory will assist in understanding runaway behavior because emotions are social motivators of behavior (Calhoun and Solomon, 1984, p. 317). The interactions that the youths report form a matrix of beliefs composed of the cultural norms and social expectations of social institutions. By studying these interactions, we begin to understand the underlying perspectives that motivate youths' runaway behavior. Theories from the sociology of emotion can amplify the details of the adolescents' decisions to run away.

Runaways' frustration mounted at not having their needs met, and at not being able to meet the expectations in the family. The decisions to run were packed with emotion. Dissecting the hitherto undiscussed socioemotional component of this response to conflict in the family, school, and community structures will deepen our understanding of this painful social phenomenon. I will show that a moral and emotional component is always present in the runaways' accounts, and a clear analysis of its role is missing from the sociological theories of deviance and delinquency.

This project began when I decided to speak to runaways to ask them how they see the problem and its solutions. I imagined that by listening carefully to runaways and to the emotional journeys they had traveled, I would get to the heart of the matter. I wanted to tell the story of running away from the perspectives of runaways themselves. I decided to find a place where I could ask runaways how they felt about running away, about their decisions to run, and about how they make sense of their decisions.

PROCEDURE: DESIGN AND METHODOLOGY

The shelter where I gathered the data on adolescent runaways was a short-term facility that could house nine residents, ages twelve to seventeen, boys and girls, who could stay a maximum of forty-five days. The shelter's residents were voluntary; that is, it was not a secured facility. The shelter participated in a closed referral system in which residents had to be referred from the Department of Social Services or the Department of Youth Services (for youth offenders) in order to be placed there. In other words, a runaway or abandoned youth could not walk up to the front door and gain admittance.

A placement at the shelter enabled staff to assess the adolescents' emotional needs, administer medications if necessary, and let them "settle down," while the county decided what to do with them next. It served as an alternative detention center for truant and other status offenders as they awaited long-term program placement. This shelter was considered a temporary holding residence—the youths arrived to wait for upcoming court dates and sentencing or to be transferred to placements in foster care or group homes. Since it was not a locked facility, this shelter did not accept extremely violent delinquent offenders. Therefore, none of the participants in this study reflected accounts of runaways who had been involved in serious and/or habitual offending behavior, such as armed robbery or capital offenses.

Each resident was assigned a social service or youth service worker, and according to these social workers, if the youth earned "points" (for "good behavior") while in residence, he or she could receive passes to visit family on weekends. When appropriate, as determined by the shelter staff and the resident's assigned social worker, family members were encouraged to visit. The shelter residents participated in house meetings, dividing up and performing household chores, group therapy, and on-site schooling or busing to outside educational institutions.

The staff of the shelter consisted of educated and trained workers—mostly people of color, mostly in their twenties, attending or graduates of local colleges in the area. The shelter was staffed twenty-four hours a day. The residents were invited by the staff to go to the local YMCA to swim and use the gym, to nearby malls, to the movies, and to parks and other nearby recreational facilities. In short, most of the youths I interviewed seemed as if they had never been treated so respectfully, or so well. One young man characterized the shelter as a "country club," and almost all made statements such as, "You're lucky if you get placed here!"

I conducted twenty-four individual interviews at the shelter during the 1993-1994 academic year. The in-depth interviews were open-ended and unstructured. I interviewed any resident who wanted to talk to me. Sometimes the staff would suggest or point out a particular youth to interview, usually because the population of the shelter changed weekly, and I might not immediately discern who was new each week. I would enter the living room area and begin asking who wanted to be interviewed. Often the youths would look at one another sideways and give nods. I overheard youths who had been interviewed previously, telling newly arrived shelter residents that "It's cool; it's OK," when referring to the interview process. This helped create a kind of "snowball" method for identifying participants. I also spent time with them just hanging out in the common living area or in the garage/clubhouse, playing pool or watching television. I observed these young adults preparing dinner with one another and ate dinner with them. I would stay to participate with them in directed activities such as Health Group, which was guided group discussions on topics such as meditation or AIDS.

To conduct the interview, each respondent and I went upstairs to the director's office for a tape-recorded conversation. We would go over the "rules" of the interview—that it was voluntary, that they could terminate it at any time, that it was confidential. I would always have the adolescent sit in the "good chair"—the director's big, white easy chair in front of the desk. I would take a smaller, lower chair. (Each time I did this, the resident's eyes would widen with wonder—"I get to sit there?") I took no written notes, relying on the tape recorder. I kept an interview schedule under a stack of blank paper in front of me and made perfunctory notes. I spoke briefly about my background and about the book I wanted to write, and then I asked the teenager to tell me about his or her experiences.

I began by asking some preliminary, icebreaker questions, such as what kind of music the teenager listened to or if he or she had a favorite movie. Then I asked the youth to tell me how he or she came to be in this shelter. I asked about school, about family members, about friends; and I asked how he or she felt about these people and places. Since I was interested in how runaways made sense of their decisions, I asked how the youth felt about the events he or she was describing, what the events meant to him or her, or how he or she came to make their decisions.

The runaways brought up a wide range of topics, and in many of the interviews, patterns emerged as each would mention the same topics as the others. Some of the issues that they shared with me included stepfamilies and foster families; smoking cigarettes; use and sale of marijuana, crack cocaine, and hallucinogenic drugs; their and their parents' drinking of alcohol; guns, death, and suicide attempts; rape, incest, and emotional violations and betrayals; pregnancy, miscarriages, and abortions; crime and encounters with the police; lying; and therapy. Each interview lasted approximately one hour.

DESCRIPTION OF THE SAMPLE

My sample included interviews with twenty-four teenagers (and two adult runaways)[13]—fifteen females (58 percent) and eleven males (42 percent).[14] A 1990 report estimates that exactly this percentage (58 percent female and 42 percent male) is a reliable approximation of the runaway population nationally (U.S. Department of Justice Fact Sheet, 1990). Participants were from varied ethnic/racial backgrounds. Of the runaways, 61 percent were white, 23 percent were Puerto Rican, and 12 percent were African American. One person described himself as Native American. The estimates for the national runaway population are as follows: 69 percent to 70 percent white, 7 percent Latino/Puerto Rican, 17 percent to 20 percent African American, and 4 percent other combined (Burgess, 1986; USGAO, 1989).[15]

Participants' ages ranged from thirteen to seventeen years old. The average age of runaways in my sample is 14.75 years old; the national average is estimated at fifteen years old (NASW, 1993). The modal age for the participants was thirteen years old, slightly younger than the national modal age, which is thought to be fifteen years old (Burgess, 1986). The youngest age at which anyone from my sample reported running away from home was eight years old, but the modal age for the first run was eleven years old. When I asked them how many times they had run away from home, 54 percent told me "so many times" or "more than six times." When I asked them how long they had been away from their parents' home or legal place of residence on this present run, 14 percent responded "one to two weeks." The rest told me from one month to two years (55 percent), or their answers were unclear (31 percent). One adult respondent reported "never" returning home after running away twenty-four years ago.

The only indicator I have of the socioeconomic background of my sample was a response to the question, "What is your mom's, your dad's, or your stepparent's job?" It appears that the majority of respondents were from homes that were disadvantaged economically. Most of the runaways (58 percent) stated low-paying, unskilled occupations or public assistance for their parents: "cleans motels," "nursing home," "in school for her GED," "on disability." Twelve percent responded with professional occupations, such as "airplane electronics" or "realtor," and 30 percent named working-class occupations, such as "plumber" or "post office," for their parents. Although a disproportionate amount of youths in my sample ran away from homes in which the chief wage earner is unemployed, on public assistance, or working in a menial job,[16] I suspect that this might be due to another social indicator—the geographical location of the shelter.

The rural setting of the shelter naturally produced a sample that disproportionately represented rural adolescents. Whereas in the national population of runaways it is estimated that nearly identical percentages of urban and rural children are represented (USGAO, 1989).[17] In this sample, 58 percent of the respondents were from rural areas, 35 percent were from nearby urban centers, and for 7 percent, it was unclear where they were from originally. It is possible that the surrounding rural regions are more economically depressed than the metropolitan regions, and that may be why this sample produced a disproportionate number from socioeconomically disadvantaged families and so few from middle-class families, compared to estimates of national averages of the runaway population.

The few runaways who were from nearby "inner cities" talked about gangs and selling crack cocaine, but the "country" kids seemed just as distrusting and angry, exhibiting similar behaviors of adolescents in conflict—smoking cigarettes, stealing cars, inappropriately sexualized behavior, ingesting drugs and alcohol. Although location may have influenced the socioeconomic situations of the families the adolescents were running away from, many of the social and emotional problems that the adolescents discussed were the same whether they were from metropolitan or rural settings.

Also discussed earlier in this chapter were national reports of proportions of runaways fleeing sexual and physical abuse. For this study, 77 percent of all respondents reported physical abuse, and 31 percent cited this as the reason that they ran away from home. Of the respondents, 35 percent reported experiencing sexual abuse, and 8 percent offered this as the cause of running away. Thirty-one percent of the runaways experienced both sexual and physical abuse in their families of origin. Furthermore, from the accounts that runaways related, and from the notes in their charts at the shelter, I concluded that it is possible that two participants (8 percent) appear to be young survivors of a rare form of abuse called ritual abuse, in which the parents participate in some type of cult worship. It is likely that these runaway children witnessed, and were participants in, ceremonies involving sexual acts, animal sacrifices, and other ritual behavior.[18]

The family structure of the runaways varied: 27 percent of the respondents ran away from homes in which their biological mothers and fathers were married and living together in intact marriages; 35 percent of the adolescents ran away from homes with a single mother heading the household; 31 percent ran away from homes with a biological parent and a stepparent (all but one of these families consisted of mothers and stepfathers). This relatively even distribution of runaways across family constitution might serve to debunk yet another myth: that single mothers cannot control their children and that an inordinate amount of runaways come from homes headed by single mothers.[19]

To organize the biographical information revealed in the interviews, I prepared tables that sorted these data for each of the twenty-six participants by the following factors: age, grade, gender, racial and ethnic designation, region of origin (rural or urban, or what state they ran away from), if they had a boy- or girlfriend (and sexual identity), any pregnancies (or girlfriends' pregnancies), any offspring, which parents were at home, siblings (at home or not, and their ages), participants' use of drugs/alcohol, if they suffered physical and/or sexual abuse, if they reported incest or stranger rape, age at first run, number of runs, length of present run, reason for present run, and mother's/father's/stepparent's age, job, and level of educational attainment. I used these sorted data to organize my understanding of the conditions of their lives that might influence runaway behavior and to present as much of this information as possible, while still protecting the identity of the runaways. Due to the necessity to protect the confidentiality of the participants, however, much of the exact details of the biographical data (except gender and ethnicity) is altered, and those "working tables" are not reproduced in this report.

CONTEMPORARY PROBLEMS
IN THE STUDY OF RUNAWAYS

It is difficult to clearly define the category runaway from reading intake interviews in shelters across the nation, inspecting social work records, and combing the literature on this topic. The dynamics of the conditions and causes for running away are so varied that clear-cut identification of the population is complicated. The U.S. Department of Justice's Juvenile Justice Division issues reports on children in five categories: runaways, throwaways, lost, injured, or missing. These last three categories form a "mixed group of children who are missing from their caretakers for a variety of reasons" (U.S. Department of Justice, 1990, p. 16). This group includes children who may have "forgotten the time, misunderstood expectations, or whose caretakers misunderstood when the children would return" and also children who "experienced physical harm, abuse or assault" in the course of their absence (U.S. Department of Justice, 1990, p. 16). Recent developments complicate the study of runaways by blurring these categories and making it difficult to identify a runaway population. Four main developments affect the identification and analysis of runaway behavior: the rise of physical and sexual abuse; the emotional makeup of the runaway; the structure of the living situations from which adolescents are running; and the differing kinds of behavior while on the run. All four of these issues influenced the analysis of my sample.

First, the prevalence of runaways' reporting physical and sexual abuse in the family has forced a shift in social service agents' perspective from seeing runaways as all "bad" and "delinquent" to seeing some of them as victims who are justified in running away from home (Janus et al., 1987, p. 17). This group of survivors is now counted differently from runaways who have not been abused and have left home because of overprotective parents or because of the appeal of the street life with their peers. The category of "abused runaways" leads to placements in foster families or juvenile facilities, at which point youths are no longer counted as runaways, but are in the juvenile social service system as foster kids, or simply as detainees in long-term facilities. The rise in abuse also affects the second issue: the emotional condition of the abused runaway.

Adolescent runaways who have been forced to run away from sexual assault and physical brutality in the family have special emotional needs that set them apart from youths who have run away from overly strict parents or for other reasons. The aftereffects of abuse are brutal. One scholar lists suicidal feelings, anger, inability to achieve intimacy and trust, anxiety, participation in delinquent and criminal activity, low self-esteem, difficulties with social contacts, inability to trust adult men, more physical ailments, fear of sex, more likely to engage in physical and verbal fights, withdrawal, seeming to be haunted, dissatisfied, depressed, lonely, and fear of being alone as some of the psychological and behavioral effects on abuse survivors that are seen in runaways (Burgess, 1986, pp. 11-13). Family reunification for runaways identified as abused is out of the question, so attempts are made to locate alternative housing for them—usually in foster care or group homes.

The third factor that prevents a clear or universal picture of runaways is the nature of the situations from which they are running. A common scenario involves runaways from foster care and group home placements.[20] These children were initially removed from the homes of their families of origin because a parent, other family member, or "friend of the family" was molesting or physically assaulting them. The social service providers place these uprooted children in foster families or in a group home. The youths may then run away from this social service placement. Some of the youths are removed from the home "unwillingly," thus not wanting to live in alternative facilities, and wish to return to the family of origin, sometimes, even if it is abusive. Other runaways report that the foster family was too strict or made arbitrary demands on them.[21] These youths who were plucked from their homes of origin are circulating within a juvenile social service network and are submerged within a population of youngsters who may have run away due to other kinds of conflict, or who may have been picked up on robbery, assault, or drug charges. In short, the category runaway, on any municipal or federal report, is not as clearly defined as it may appear when first approaching the topic.

The last issue that impedes the development of a cohesive sociological theory of runaway behavior is the variation in the behavior of youths on the run. Not only are runaways committing petty crimes such as shoplifting and vandalism; they are increasingly committing armed assault, using and selling of controlled narcotic substances, engaging in prostitution, and committing murder. Nationally, 30 percent of runaways are reported to be "in trouble with the juvenile justice system" (NASW, 1993). One California police lieutenant explains this development:

There is no way a twelve-year-old can legitimately survive on the streets of Los Angeles. They have to have the necessities of life. For most, the only thing they can do is sell their bodies. (U.S. Department of Justice, 1989, p. 3)

So these youths, too, lose their original designation of runaway and come to be listed as "offender," thus complicating the identification of a clear-cut demographic category of runaways. In my sample, by the time I had interviewed seven of the respondents, they were no longer primarily considered runaways, although it was revealed in the interview that before the adolescents were apprehended by the police, they had run away from home.

CONCLUSION

The runaway problem is widespread, and misperceptions about runaways abound. Between 1 and 2 million runaways are on the streets and in the runaway shelter network nationwide. Common assumptions about runaways include that their main problem is they are psychopathological and have personal problems that therapy would solve, or they come from low-income, single-family homes that cannot discipline them well enough. In this chapter, I suggest that the most effective approach to the runaway problem is to use ideas from interaction and conflict perspectives and from the sociology of emotion, which seeks to include an understanding of individual runways, their families and social settings, and the interactions that make up their behavior and experience.

I conducted twenty-four interviews with individual runaways and spent several months participating in activities with youths at a rural shelter, which formed the basis of the information analyzed in this study. All interviews were conducted in private and with informed consent of the participants. The participants told me their life stories, the events that led up to them being at a youth shelter, and how they felt about these experiences. The youths were surprisingly open and forthcoming with intimate details of their experiences, although in a few clear instances, they exercised their option not to disclose specifics of certain events. This research reports the runaway experience from the viewpoint of runaways. Due to the limitations in scope of the project, I was not able to interview parents, relatives, and social workers of the participants. However, after meeting rigorous research standards designed to protect human subjects, I was granted access to their files at the shelter, which are completed by licensed social workers and police agents and do provide corroborating evidence to many of the events that are self-reported by the runaways.

Wherever possible, I present these data from the files with the runaways' accounts to attempt to address the obvious difficulty for researchers who rely on self-reported data from their participants. Striking a balance between accepting the youths' narratives as "true" and needing corroboration was key. The issue of believing youths' accounts has further profound and complex implications in the study of young people in conflict. For example, the authors of one study of runaways make the alarming suggestion that parents were blaming the child for running away and denying abuse and conflict to escape detection as perpetrators of abuse (Janus et al., 1987, p. 48). Social service agents, for differing reasons—funding issues, disagreements over social service provision techniques, blurring of definitions of sexual and physical abuse—may disbelieve the accounts of teenage runaways or assess that runaways are exaggerating and insist on returning youths to their families (Powers and Jaklitsch, 1989, p. 10). Issues of bias against taking youths' stories seriously, or accepting them wholeheartedly, are key when studying youths because important determinations are made about their living situations based on these accounts. Elements of this discussion are developed throughout this book.

In Chapter 2, I will present the theoretical frameworks that underlie the ideas presented in this chapter.

Screaming

I wish I could run away . . . Screaming and Screaming, I wish
I could just get out of here.

"Shut the fuck up, I heard you already, why do you keep on
repeating yourself, do you just like to hear yourself or
what!" Is what I shouted.

Walking in the room . . . Screaming and Screaming, I wish I
could just leave.

"You disrespectful little bitch, all you care about is yourself,
nothing and no one else!" Is what my mom yelled.

Slamming the door, telling my dad what had happened, my
dad walked out of his room . . .

Screaming and Bamm! . . .

"Now try talking back to your mother, with a cracked head,
you dirty bitch!" Is what my dad hollered.

I don't know what happened . . . Screaming and Screaming,
now thinking to myself, why did he just slam my head into
the wall.

Fuck'n asshole! What if I did that to him?!

I wish he would understand . . . Screaming and Screaming, all
I hear is loud shrieks coming from my lungs, after seeing
the blood run down my face.

The blood is still falling and I am now crying from the pain . . .
Screaming and Screaming, another personal thought:

Get Out!, Get Out! Why don't you leave! You're stupid, look
at what he just did to you! Get away from here . . . that was
the day I decided to leave.

Valentina Sedeno

Chapter 2

Running Away:
Theories of Emotion and Deviance

I said, "I don't even look like him, and I don't look like you, so maybe I'm adopted!" And she went ballistic! She turned around and she started kickin', punchin', swearin', bitin'. I just got her off me and "bitch-slapped" her and went, "Wow, that's the first time I ever hit my mom!" She ran out of the room, and I slammed the door right behind her and locked it. I stayed up there trying to get . . . I just sat there, and I thought, "Oh my God, I hit my mother. Holy Shit! I can't believe I hit my mom!" And I just jumped out my bedroom window and ran. [From his files: "Broke his mother's nose five months ago."]

Roy, age sixteen

INTRODUCTION

In recent decades, human service workers, social scientists, and community activists have studied the problem of runaway teenagers and offered solutions. Although social work has produced voluminous articles, studies, and treatment approaches, psychology and psychiatry have advanced medical models, and civic and urban organizations have responded by funding shelters and group homes, social science has not yielded a comprehensive or cohesive perspective. Most sociologists have treated running away as juvenile delinquent behavior, and adolescent runaways are most often discussed under the rubric of sociological deviance. However, the sociology literature does analyze adolescent runaway behavior from other approaches. Scholars have examined the problem from a symbolic interactionist perspective (Wilkinson, 1987; Palenski, 1984) and social psychological viewpoints (Brennan, Huizinga, and Elliott, 1978), a conflict perspective (Janus et al., 1987), and through the lens of deviance theories (Nye, 1985; Reiss, 1951).

In this chapter, I will present ideas from the sociology of emotion and give an overview of major theoretical perspectives that sociologists have applied to runaway behavior: interactionist and conflict perspectives and control theory from the sociology of deviance. I will explain the advantages of applying ideas from the sociology of emotion to these other analyses of runaway behavior to amplify our current understanding of the problem.

EMOTION THEORY

Emotion and Its Role in Social Life

Emotion has been considered in many different lights by psychologists, philosophers, and, more recently, sociologists. Definitions of emotion range from the Aristotelian perspective that considers emotion as a cognitive assessment of any given situation to the Jamesian viewpoint that sees it as purely physiological sensation (Calhoun and Solomon, 1984, p. 3). Emotion can be presented as consisting of three dimensions: the physiological feeling/sensation, the recognition of the sensations and cognitions about them, and emotional action or behavior (Calhoun and Solomon, 1984, p. 14). A sociological definition of emotion might consider emotion as a sensate experience that derives from a social condition or situation. It would include a cognitive thought process in which the actor recognizes what he or she feels and is thus motivated to act or behave based on those sensations and decisions about the means of expression (whether by crying, sulking, laughing, hugging, yelling, or, possibly, running away). Sociologist Arlie Hochschild defines emotion as "conscious awareness of bodily cooperation with an idea, thought, or attitude and the label attached to that awareness" (1975, p. 300). Sociology views emotion as a social phenomenon because feelings evolve from interactions within the cultural norms of social structures (Hochschild, 1975; Kemper, 1978; Shott, 1979). Hochschild (1983) notes:

> Emotion . . . is a biologically given sense, and our most important one. Like other senses—hearing, touch, and smell—it is a

means by which we know about our relation to the world, and it is therefore crucial for the survival of human beings in group life. Emotion is unique among the senses, however, because it is related not only to an orientation toward action but also toward cognition. (p. 219)

Thus, emotion plays a key role in human exchange and interaction—not only motivating our behavior but also our understanding. Hochschild (1975) presents two models of emotion: organismic (biological) and interactionist (social). Emotion theorists fall into these two loosely located opposing areas on a continuum. On the one side, naturalists (organismic oriented) argue that emotions well up from our biological depths and are sensation- and physiologically driven. On the other side of the continuum, social constructionists (interactionists) describe emotions as culturally construed, adopted, and refined, depending on a dominant sociocultural environment. Scholars leaning toward cognitive and evaluative emotion theories more readily adopt this acquisitionist viewpoint because cognitive-evaluative theories stress the decisional component of our emotional experience. In other words, we feel a sensation, we interpret it, and that evaluation determines our behavior. Hochschild points out that "in the interactional model, social factors enter into the very formulation of emotions, through codification, management, and expression" (1983, p. 207). Social interaction and social process play a role in the creation of emotion itself.

The difference between a psychological interpretation of emotion and the way that sociologists view emotion lies, not in definitions of emotion as a sensate experience, but more in the formation, expression, and role or use of emotion. All people have feelings, but sociologists do not view this as individual, solitary phenomena. Feelings are created socially, and feelings motivate social behavior. Theorist Susan Shott suggests that a thorough understanding of social behavior requires the "study of the role of emotion in social life" (1979, p. 1318). Shott offers a symbolic interactionist conceptualization of emotion:

The actions of individuals are influenced by their internal states and impulses in addition to external events and stimuli, for actor's perceptions and interpretations are shaped by the former as well as the latter (Hewitt 1976, p. 47). Physiological or psychological impulses, once noticed, form the beginning of an act and motivate the actor toward its consummation (Mead 1938, pp. 3-8, 23-25). In no sense does the impulse determine the act, but it is a significant component of action and adds to its dynamic character. (1979, p. 1321)

So, not only is emotion socially derived, but it can motivate behavior. Seeing emotion as "a significant component of action" is key to a sociological understanding of the effects of emotion. It is not a biological coincidence that people share certain emotional behavioral responses, depending on their social settings. Interactionist theorists analyze the social influence of the formation of emotions, and the social influence of emotions on behavior, by evaluating groups of people in similar circumstances responding with similar behaviors. Culturally contrived and socially learned, emotions play a key role in guiding the actions of groups of people who find themselves under similar conditions.

Emotion and Runaway Teenagers

Emotion is a key influence in meaning construction and decision making for youths who run away from home. Emotions are "urgent judgments; emotional responses are emergency behavior" (Calhoun and Solomon, 1984, p. 319). Sociologist Jack Katz (1988), in his groundbreaking work on crime, uses emotion theory to amplify an understanding of some of the motivations to deviate. Although crime differs considerably from runaway behavior, Katz' careful explication of the role of "moral" emotions—cynicism, humiliation, and vengeance—nevertheless opens the door to a deeper understanding of the social effects of emotion on our behavior.

Emotion animates the perspectives of the runaways and influences their behavior. When they run away, adolescents report feeling more emotionally connected to their friends (Brennan, Huizinga, and Elliott, 1978, p. 282). Teenage runaways flee families in conflict and often end up with their peers. They form emotional connections to one another—following Scheff's maxim that "the maintenance of social bonds is the most crucial human motive" (1990, p. 4). Emotion theory helps explicate the meaning of the runaways' reports that they feel more connected with, and interested in, their peers than their parents, teachers, and other adults (Brennan, Huizinga, and Elliott, 1978, p. 282). I will apply emotion theory with other important sociological perspectives, discussed next, to the data garnered in the interviews with runaways to broaden our understanding of the runaway phenomenon.

INTERACTIONISM

Symbolic interactionism is an interpretive analysis of microinteractions that uses a complex social psychological framework, focusing on the way people "act toward, respond to, and influence one another" (Robertson, 1987, p. 20). Interactionist theorists analyze the interplay between individuals and the social structures they inhabit by studying the processes and meaning-making constructions of interpersonal exchanges. Interactionist theorist Herbert Blumer describes three premises of interactionist theory:

> human beings act toward things on the basis of the meanings that the things have for them, . . . that the meaning of such things is derived from the social interaction that one has with one's fellow . . . and that these meanings are handled in, and modified through, an interpretive process used by the person in dealing with things he encounters. (1969, p. 2)

Sociology is a science that connects individual acts with the social world in which they occur. Blumer's theories of meaning construction are key to a sociological understanding of how actors, such as adolescent runaways, construct their worlds and live within them.

To understand and explain runaway behavior, it will be useful to apply interactionist perspectives; this includes taking into account runaways' interpretations and responses to their experiences in their families and other institutions. As Palenski notes, "For interactionists, the significance of meaning is that it guides action" (1984, p. 32). Paying close attention to the stories of their interactions with parents, peers, teachers, social workers, and police reveals the ways that runaways make sense of their worlds and make decisions about how to act in those environments.

Blumer (1969) suggests that actors derive the meanings of the social interactive events in their lives by "handling and modifying" the meanings through an interpretative process. This process is not solely cognitive: it contains an emotion domain. Focusing on the emotional component of the "interpretive process" that Blumer offers will reveal important patterns of behavior in the runaway experience. Using an interactionist perspective and applying emotion analysis to the details of runaways' stories penetrates the decision-making process that runaways use in assessing the ways they can best resolve their dilemmas.

Whereas the interactionist viewpoint zeros in on the exchanges between people whose microinteractions create and maintain the large structures in society, such as family, schools, and community, a conflict perspective widens the sociological lens and captures larger structural tensions, as well as the power dynamics in these structures.

CONFLICT PERSPECTIVE

Conflict perspective, derived from various Marxist theoretical approaches, is another sociological approach that provides insight into the runaway problem. Conflict theorists view human interactions and social exchanges as struggles over material and symbolic resources. Studying the dynamics of power between social groups, conflict theorists look at social problems and ask, "Who's interests are being served by the outcomes of this situation?" (Robertson, 1987, p. 20). Conflict theorists consider conflictual social processes as the means by which people organize and redistribute material resources (such as capital and property) and symbolic wealth (such as power and prestige). They view change as normal and expected: life is an unending competitive tension that eventually (and hopefully) yields improvements for individuals and society. Sociologist Ian Robertson explains that:

> conflict theorists regard the . . . vision of a general consensus on values as pure fiction: what actually happens, they argue, is that the powerful coerce the rest of the population into compliance and conformity. (1987, p. 20)

So, at times, the "rest of the population" counterresponds in non-compliance and nonconformity, causing growth and change in the values, norms, and morals of a community. Applying a conflict perspective specifically to runaway behavior yields rich results.

Youths can be seen to be in a subordinate and powerless position inside the family and other social structures, such as the educational institutions where they are students subject to the regulations set by teachers and administrators (Brennan, Huizinga, and Elliott, 1978, p. 81). Tension mounts as youths struggle to meet the expectations of families or teachers. Some of the situations in the families are unbearable—physical and sexual abuse occurs at an alarming rate. As one theorist states:

> Advocates of this position believe that it is reasonable to ex-pect youths to try to escape from these environments. (Janus et al., 1987, p. 49)

Young people report feeling that their lives are overstructured and arbitrarily regulated (Ianni, 1989, p. 7) and respond to these power struggles in the family or at school with strong emotions. Some resolve their crises by running away. They feel powerless in their subordinate positions in social institutions, and I will show that their reactions—running away—to perceived maltreatment in rela-tionships within those institutions are acts of insubordination and rebellious behavior.

Although the conflict perspective applied to runaway behavior yields interesting results, a cautionary note is in order here. On the one hand, it can be documented that legal power in America does not rest in the hands of young people. At the same time, however, con-temporary United States reflects a youth-oriented culture to a great extent. Family theorists trace the changes in notions of authority in the family over time and find that in modern middle-class families, negotiation and a certain amount of reciprocity is expected between parents and children (Levine and White, 1994, p. 286; Montemayor, 1990, p. 131). It is likely that—with variations because of factors such as race and ethnicity, socioeconomics, and religion—most American families do not have authoritarian, "respect-your-elders-automatically" types of expectations. But this study is about families in conflict, and the participants are youths who are experiencing extreme trauma and who report perceiving that they are being treated unfairly. Therefore, the conflict perspective assists by illuminating key notions of powerlessness and rebellion in their runaway experience.

From the conflict perspective, an analysis of the role of emotion in runaway behavior reveals an emotional "time bomb" for adolescent runaways. I will argue that the rage, disappointment, fear, and sadness that these teens report will support the construction of runaway behavior as emotional behavior that seeks to alleviate tension produced by struggles to conform. The sociology of emotion provides an analysis of the feelings produced from interactions due to the inequalities of the social structures and examines acts of insubordination and rebellion against unfair treatment. Running away includes an emotional struggle that conflict perspective alone does not explain.

The sociology of emotion reveals essential aspects of the conflict perspective of runaway behavior, even though emotion theorists disagree about the origin of feelings. Some theorists posit that feelings are produced in social institutions themselves; others see emotion as stemming from interactions with social norms and cultural expectations of the institutions—the "feeling rules" that guide the norms (Hochschild, 1983, p. 18). For example, feelings may run high in the family interactions of runaways, but "families" per se do not determine runaway behavior. Emotion is produced in the interactions among family members as they work out the meaning of their lives with one another. However, these interactions are not among equals and can be analyzed in terms of the power arrangements of the actors. Shott cautions that interactions cannot exactly predict behavior:

> social structures and normative regulations form a framework of human action rather than its determinant, shaping behavior without dictating it. (1979, p. 1321)

Sensation theorist Theodore Kemper disagrees. Kemper offers an analysis of emotions that:

> looks to an important link with biology and the physiological concomitants of emotions; rejects the view that cultural norms

determine emotions; looking instead to social structure and to the outcomes of social relations; and, while accepting the constructionists' view that emotions depend on how the situation has been defined, unlike them, offers concrete, empirically grounded formulations for how actors define situations. (1981, p. 337)

Kemper uses the term "social structure" to mean the "vertical arrangement of actors" in relation to dimensions of power and status.

For runaways, almost all adults with whom are involved—parents, teachers, school officials, pimps, pornographers, employers, police, and social workers—are their hierarchical superiors. Almost everyone, other than peers, siblings, other runaways, and "delinquents," has some kind of structural power over them. These power imbalances influence emotional life. Emotions, such as rage, disappointment, indignation, and fear, derive from these interactions and power struggles. Kemper emphatically states that "power and status relationships, not social norms, produce emotions" (1981, p. 339). His provocative idea is that:

> it is what our fellow participants do to us and what we do to them—the social relations that constitute the existing social structure—that evoke our emotions. (1981, p. 344)

I will show how emotion theory highlights the role of anger and resentment in teenagers rebelling against "what our fellow participants do to us." Sociologist Thomas Scheff, self-critical of his early conceptualization of consensus, now adds that:

> it was entirely cognitive, since it concerned only beliefs and perceptions of beliefs. It omitted entirely a component which is easily as important as beliefs and perceptions and *may even predominate over them when there is conflict: emotions.* (1990, p. 74; emphasis mine)

It is just such an emotional conflict—about overthrowing consensus and all the cultural norms that keep them at home, in the family, and in the educational system—that teenage runaways experience when they decide to run away. Applying the sociology of emotion in the analysis of the emotional conflicts they experience will fill in missing connections in our understanding of runaways' motivations to run.

Using the sociology of emotion to study the interactions between runaways and the norms of family, school, legal, and other social systems in which they engage broadens the explanations of runaway behavior that sociologists offer. The interactionist perspective allows us to closely evaluate the interactions where the norms, expectations, and morals regarding the family structure are engineered. The conflict viewpoint reminds us that these relationships and interactions are not equal—that a power dynamic is at work which influences the interactions, and thus the feelings, produced by these inequitable arrangements. Both the interactionist and conflict viewpoints consider the tensional interaction between the runaways and their attempts to conform to the expectations of the social structures in society as central to explaining runaway behavior. Control theory is also useful in explaining runaway behavior because it reveals the details of the social connections that keep adolescents attached to society.

CONTROL THEORY

One other sociological explanation I use to analyze runaway behaviors is a deviance analysis termed control theory. Sociologists have viewed running away from home as deviant behavior, and control theory is often cited to explain it (Nye, 1980, 1985; Hirschi, 1985; Brennan, Huizinga, and Elliott, 1978). Control theory is really more about conformity than about deviance. It is formed upon a Hobbesian premise that people need to be constrained in order to conform to society because living in antisocial lawlessness is a natural state for human beings. For example, control theories would not question, "Why do runaways run away?" but would ask, instead, "Why don't all teenagers run away?" Therefore, this theory asserts that "most delinquent behavior is the result of insufficient social control, broadly defined" (Nye, 1985, p. 245).

Social control theory is predicated on the idea that conformity is held in place by social connectedness and sanctions. Criminologist Travis Hirschi developed a social bond theory, stating that "delinquent acts result when an individual's bond to society is weak or broken" (1985, p. 257). Hirschi elaborates four elements of the social bond: attachment, involvement, commitment, and belief.

Attachment

Hirschi argues that people conform to the norms of their communities because they care about what other people think of them. French sociologist Émile Durkheim stated, "We are moral beings to the extent that we are social beings" (1961, p. 8), and as Hirschi offers, this "may be interpreted to mean that we are moral beings to the extent that we have internalized the norms of society" (1985, p. 258). For adolescents contemplating running away, being attached to their families, their schools, and their peers has moral and emotional dimensions. Hirschi notes that:

> The process of becoming alienated from others often involves, or is based on, active interpersonal conflict. Such conflict could easily supply a reservoir of *socially derived* hostility sufficient to account for the aggressiveness of those whose attachments to others have been weakened. (1985, p. 258)

Because we are attached to others' opinions of us, we develop morals and conform to the norms of our cultures. These social bonds of attachment are constructed emotionally and have an emotional character:

> Without emotion, there would be no values, rather only rules and methods without inspiration. It is emotion, not reflection, that most endows the world with meaning. (Calhoun and Solomon, 1984, p. 40)

This idea is central to my argument. Morals, norms, and expectations—in Calhoun's and Solomon's sense—are more than just a set of regulations dictated by a social contract. They become the rules that govern and connect us in families and social structures and are imbued with emotion. Therefore, many of the struggles over connection or rupture of social bonds between people and in families are moral struggles—full of emotion—and can be seen as conflicts over society's rules.

Brennan and colleagues (1978) suggest that the element of attachment implies a personal and moral link that encompasses the internalization of societal expectations (p. 62), and Hirschi's (1985) original notion of attachment also leaves the emotional component implicit. I believe an emotional component exists, and I will examine it explicitly. I argue that the emotional domain in the social bond becomes quite clear in runaways' struggles to conform with expectations and in their decision-making processes. I will show that when runaways seem to throw off the connections that link them to society, there is an intense moral and emotional rupture in their attachment to what they perceive to be oppressive structures (and a simultaneous search for connection to perceived "friendly" structures). Running away is a process of disattachment and reattachment—and it is an emotional process.

Commitment

Hirschi explicates his notion of commitment as the "rational component to conformity" (1985, p. 259). His argument is that the social bond contains, as Zide describes it, the "commitment to pursue conventional means and goals" (Zide, 1990, p. 38). Hirschi believes that people enjoy their pursuit of a conventional goal and, thus, weigh out the risks and assess the possible losses of committing a deviant act. He writes that "attachment is . . . conscience, commitment is . . . common sense" (1985, p. 260). It would seem that Hirschi is saying that attachment is emotional and commitment is cognitive, but I believe that commitment is also imbued with feelings.

This element of the social bond is weakened when runaways perceive that their attempts to commit to normative structures such as families are thwarted because those attempts take place inside of families in intense conflict. Runaways may then make a "common sense" decision to leave what they consider an unbearable or abusive family situation. Deciding to commit to a family structure may represent a cognitive, rational assessment, but any decision to pursue or turn away from a goal may be motivated by submerged emotion (Bedford, 1984, p. 278). Embedded within the narratives of runaways is decision making fraught with emotions. When expectations are continually unmet, emotions such as disappointment result, and the commitment in a social bond may weaken.

Involvement

Control theory holds that delinquency results because youths are not involved in normative activities linking them to the structures of the dominant culture—in families, at schools, work, or other social arenas—and thus the social bonds are weakened. Hirschi's (1985) notion of involvement is that if people spend their time and energy involved in socially acceptable normative behaviors, such as family activities, work, and school, then it will be difficult for them to find time or energy to participate in deviant behavior.

Involvement in the dominant normative culture has been a subject of study for deviance theorists since the inception of deviance theory. As Sutherland and Cressey (1985) point out, "criminal behavior is learned behavior," and deviance is most often learned in intimate groups (p. 180). Social worker Marilyn Zide noted that bonding to normative society is:

> a condition that develops between an individual and society when individuals perceive that the society is important to their well-being. In other words, deviant behavior, such as running away, would be avoided because it would jeopardize the individual's sense of well-being. (1990, p. 37)

Involvement in conventional activities might also assist adolescents in placing family and peer conflict in context—giving them perspective and helping them to prioritize their problems. However, "conventional activities"—effective schools, healthy associations with peers, and normative community structures—*must be available* if they are to focus teenagers' attentions on normative activities.

Living in emotionally, physically, or sexually abusive or humiliating families in which a great deal of energy is spent fighting and yelling does not encourage runaways to stay involved in home life (or at schools or in community settings). Being involved in peer relationships that are emotionally satisfying, nurturing, and helpful pulls runaways outside of their homes. Hirschi notes that involvement in conventional settings takes up the time and energy of society's members. Using the sociology of emotion to focus on the feeling reports of the runaways and the meanings that the feelings have for them will show that feelings influence involvement, and the more emotionally satisfying bonds with peers draw runaways' involvement away from families, schools, and community agencies that are perceived by runaways as not meeting their needs.

Belief

Adolescents who have strong social bonds to the institutions in society share "conventional and similarly-held beliefs" with other conforming members (Zide, 1990, p. 38).

Hirschi's belief framework rests on this configuration:

> a person's beliefs in the moral validity of norms are, for no teleological reason, weakened. The probability that he will commit a delinquent act is therefore increased. When and if he commits a delinquent act, we may justifiably use the weakness of his beliefs in explaining it, but no special motivation is required to explain either the weakness of his beliefs, or, perhaps, his delinquent act. (1985, p. 263)

Emotion plays a role in the formation and erosion of moral bonds (Calhoun and Solomon, 1984, p. 21) that form our belief systems. Beliefs are imbued with emotion—think of the mixture of feelings and ideas that people have toward abortion, or nationalism, for example. Motivations and decisions have an emotional domain (Shott, 1979, p. 1321) and influence actions that reflect beliefs. Emotions also can modify beliefs through feeling work (Hochschild, 1983). Hochschild describes this work: "sometimes we try to stir up a feeling we wish we had, and at other times we try to block or weaken a feeling we wish we did not have" (1983, p. 43).

The bonds of belief are loosened if adolescents feel that their parents' behavior is less than something they can acceptably believe in—especially if adolescents are subjected to abuse, fighting, unfair treatment, and feeling angry, sad, hurt, rejected, and continually negative about their family lives. The emotional life of runaways will affect their belief systems. I will argue that adolescents' "beliefs in the moral validity of the norms" in the family are weakened by the conflict experienced in the family, and this weakened belief influences their decisions to run away.

Control theory offers the analysis that runaway behavior is exhibited when social bonds that tie adolescents to societal structures are weakened or broken. The sociology of emotion can specifically identify the effective elements of social bonds and illuminate the loosening of bonds by analyzing data surrounding runaway behavior, including accounts of life stories of runaways. Studying the role of emotion in the social bond experience for runaways will widen the opportunity for parents and concerned adults to comprehend and interpret the meaning that their behavior holds for runaways. It will also enable us to assist youths in understanding themselves and their own behavior.

CONCLUSION

By using emotion theory to examine the feeling component in runaway behavior, I will flesh out a picture of these frightened and incorrigible youths. I will show that emotions such as anger, fear, resentment, and hurt motivate runaway behavior. I will argue that running away is a culturally contrived process for adolescents, stimulated by emotional reactions and interactions in the family, among their peers, with their teachers, and with community agents. I will use emotion theory to show that running away consists of emotional and moral crises of trust, tempered by the proscriptive feeling rules of social bonds. By paying attention to the details of runaway teenagers' emotional lives, I develop a new understanding of how these young people—using resilient, innovative (but not always successful) methods—respond to their perceived powerlessness and stratification within families and in wider social arenas.

The following two chapters contain the life stories of youths who participated in this study. The conflict and interactionist perspectives of the deviance and emotion theories will help us understand the barrage of emotional expressions of anger, disappointment, invalidation, powerlessness, and rebellion that the youths share. Frustrated and frustrating, the youths plead their cases and show their "bad attitudes" in hopes of finding redress. By listening very carefully to their protests and triumphs, these youths can teach us about the courage to challenge conflict.

Inner Strength

I was an honor roll student, but also an alcoholic.
I had a lot of friends, but no trust.
I depended on no one; they depended on me.
I was eleven, but treated and acted like I was twenty-one.
My dad beat me, because he wanted to show control.
I didn't cry, so he felt powerless.
I fought for no other reason, but to feel pain.
I cut myself, because I was numb.
I didn't share my feelings, because no one asked.
I never said I'm sorry, because I didn't have to.
I manipulated, because I knew how.
I was strong, because I couldn't be weak.
I was a mother, and it wasn't by choice.
I imagined, because I wanted to get away.
I was sad, because there wasn't anything to be happy about.
I made goals, because no one was going to make them for me.
I couldn't cry, because I didn't get loved.
I observed, because I wasn't allowed to speak.
I survived, because I am a fighter.
I drank and did drugs, because I wasn't supposed to remember.

Valentina Sedeno

Chapter 3

Running Away
and the Socioemotional Bond

My mom thought I smoked pot. So she's like, "Where are your cigarettes? Where are they? Where's your dope—your other cigarettes?" I got really mad and [slight laugh] I punched her and she threw me down and she was like, "Don't FUCK with me!" I got out of the room and she tried it again. When she finally let go of me and . . . um . . . threw me downstairs and she said, "I'm going to go downstairs and you're going to stay up here," until she turned around and said, "Oh by the way, I'm putting a CHINS[1] on your ass!" And I said, "Good, then maybe they can get me out of this hellhole!" She said, "Well, if they don't, I'll throw you out!" I said, "If you want me to leave, then I'll leave right now . . . " She said, "Fine!" and I ran next door and called. . . . [Suffered physical abuse by her mother and her mother's boyfriend. She's in the shelter because she stabbed a girl at her school.]

Megan, age seventeen

INTRODUCTION: THE SOCIAL BOND
IS AN EMOTIONAL CONNECTION

Social control theory posits that people are connected to one another through powerful mutual bonds of expectations as they interact in groups. For adolescents, as social bonds weaken or break, delinquent behaviors (such as running away) can result (Nye, 1985,

p. 246). Youths struggle with the moral and emotional implications of these bonds through interactions in families, among their peers, in schools, and in community institutions. Runaways run from families because they are disappointed by differences between their expectations for their parents' behavior and their perceptions of their parents' actual behavior. Social bonds between parent and child become significantly diminished, if not destroyed, in some families, and runaways flee. Youths attempt to strengthen bonds with peers, at school, or in community services, always searching to be connected in social institutions to other people.

Emotion holds bonds in place, and interactions between individual and group structures through norms, values, and mores bond the individual to the social structure. An emotional dimension is central to both social bonds and social interactions (Calhoun and Solomon, 1984, p. 7; Schott, 1979, p. 1318; Scheff, 1990, p. 7). Hirschi (1985) describes social bonds as encompassing attachment, involvement, commitment, and belief. Social bonds are our connectedness to social structures through the norms, values, morals, and expectations that guide our behavior. They are our emotional and moral motivation to meet those norms. Yet, social bonds are not automatic, nor are they static. Rather, through interactions, people derive, create, and destroy social bonds. When we observe the condition of bonds, we see that they fluctuate—build and weaken, rupture, at times beyond repair, and strengthen and heal. Running away is one form of an emotional disconnection of the social bond.

By conceptualizing actors' expectations of normal behavior and observing what happens in relationships when the expectations are not met, it is possible to observe dynamics of social connectedness. Many expectations are assumed and unspoken. For example, in a family, children might expect that parents will protect them from harm, guide them safely through the world, and accept them and approve of them. Children may also expect that parents will provide them with food, a warm place to sleep, and the basic necessities of life. Parents might assume that children will obey and love them. When expectations are met, parents and children feel positive emotions within families, and the social bond is strengthened. But when people are disappointed by the behavior of those with whom they interact, and their conventional expectations remain unfulfilled, the bond is weakened, and they begin to question it or regard it as ineffectual.

In this chapter, I will show that for adolescents, running away involves an emotional process that includes the rupture of social and emotional connections, which are broken when the expectations within families are not met. Meanwhile, emotional connections may simultaneously strengthen in other areas, such as among peers. The struggles chronicled in runaways' interviews reveal an emotional battle to understand and comply with what they perceive as the expectations rooted in the social structures in which they interact: families, peers, school, and community networks, such as legal and social service systems. Runaway behavior involves crises of trust: runaways withdraw loyalty from people in one area of their lives and reassign it to others, in a meaningful search for trusting relationships. Social bonds and emotional attachments are developed or dissolved by the youths and by the people in their lives in dynamic assessments of, and searches for, safe relationships in which to connect emotionally.

This chapter begins with a brief discussion about uncovering the language of emotion through conversation and observation. The rest of the chapter is divided into four sections that show how changes in runaways' emotional connectedness to their families influence their motivation to run away. Part I begins by showing how the family bond weakens. Part II contains a discussion of how the family bond ruptures; the consequence is running away. Part III includes a look at the disheartening conditions that create ruptures in families so severe or final that they are beyond repair or rapprochement. Finally, Part IV presents stories of repairs of the family covenant that led to healing and reunion among family members. This includes a section outlining examples of the fluid nature of the shifts in bonds—how they form and weaken as runaways relate to wider social structures in life outside of the family, among their peers, at school, and in the community. I will argue that social connections are fluid and dynamic—not static—and that in their daily interactions with parents, siblings, peers, police, and social workers, the runaways' stories clearly reflect the flexible strengthening and weakening of social bonds.[2] I use the sociology of emotion to explicate a picture of the activity of the social bond.

"EMOTION TALK":
FINDING THE SOCIOLOGY OF EMOTION

Emotion is intangible and self-defined and, therefore, difficult to research. Sociologist Arlie Hochschild (1975) notes that "feelings might seem impossible to capture in the loose net of sociological instruments," and that:

> sociologists should attend to the actor's own definition of his or her feelings in order to find out how emotion vocabularies are used, what inner experiences they refer to, and what social situations or rules call them forth or squash them out. (p. 284)

Hochschild's method is essential to understanding the stories of runaways. The emotional life that runaways shared in their accounts is located as much in the way they said things—their posture, body movements, tone of voice, and rhythmic patterns of speech—as in what they said. For example, Jean,[3] a tense, frightened fifteen-year-old white girl, relates an overwhelming and tragic story of incest and abuse.

Underweight, with tiny fever blisters around her mouth, she hugged a teddy bear throughout the interview. Jean came from the rural part of a southeastern state approximately 400 miles from Massachusetts. Jean was determined to travel very far to escape her physically and sexually abusive familial situation. She had gone north in search of a relative who lived in this region. She talked in her interview about her relations with a former twenty-seven-year-old boyfriend; she had never been pregnant. Both her mother and stepfather lived at home with three young siblings, but Jean said that among the four marriages and remarriages of her parents and stepparents, there were over a dozen children. An older sister had run away from home a year before she did. Her forty-three-year-old mother, a high school graduate, owned a small shoe store, and her stepfather was a sixty-eight-year-old contractor in the construction industry and a college graduate. She ran away for the first time when she was thirteen years old, had run "many times," and hadn't been back home in "a long time." Jean disclosed that she had been raped twice by different males in the preceding year, but the major feature of Jean's story was the physical and sexual abuse she suffered at the hands of her drunken stepfather.

In an earlier part of this interview, Jean had described her stepfather's sexual abuse. Discussing the chaos in her family life, she spoke quickly and matter-of-factly about her memories:

> I've had a really messed up life because my mom and dad are stupid and dumb. . . . I ran away from my parents house about two years ago when I was thirteen years old. It was very abusive at my mom's and dad's house. Physically, emotionally, abusive. Like my second father's crazy—he was crazy! He's this total alcoholic and a big pothead and all that stuff. He had a bunch of guns and whenever he was drunk—Oh my God! He'd chase after us! . . . he'd run around and chase after us with guns! Everyday he'd go out drinking! He'd come home and my mom would go out and he would just do shit . . . and I was in there and disgusted, and the kids would watch him do this shit to me. And they couldn't do anything 'cause they are three and four and six years old, and there was no telephone, and where could I go? Could I just take the kids and run? That's why I didn't stay there—I ran away with my best friend. I'm like, "To hell with you!" and so I run out the front door, and I'm running down the street to my best friend's . . .

Jean referred to the incident when her "second father" was sexually assaulting her in front of her trapped younger siblings—but where are the "feeling words" in this passionate account? Except for the word "disgusted," there are no specific words of emotion. However, if reread carefully, within the phrase, "To hell with you!" lies "I am furious," "This hurts," "I'm confused," "I'm terrified." Her voice was tight and quiet and her leg twitched whenever she mentioned her stepfather, yet the words she chose when describing how she came to be in a youth shelter were not sophisticated articulations of emotional experiences. The young people I interviewed used phrases without an "emotion word" in them, but many used linguistic expressions and phrases rife with feelings of fear, rage, hurt, and confusion, as these examples demonstrate:

"I couldn't handle it, so I ran away!" (Roy, frightened, getting beaten by his mother)

"I'd get so sick of it that I just split!" (Anne, angry, being kicked by her mother)

"I couldn't take it anymore!" (Eva, frustrated, not being allowed to go out of her house)

"I just got so sick and tired of going through what he wanted me to do and what he wanted me to be!" (Eric, hurt, about his father's constant judgment and direction)

"And I just said, 'Forget it!' and left." (Stacey, angry, never having permission to go out of the house in the evening)

"I didn't like it, so I ran away!" (Roy, confused, after witnessing his mother beat his little brother)

"Don't feel like nothin." (LaWanda, hurt, not having her mother's love)

"It don't bother me none." (Michael, hurt, not having his father's love)

"Bam! Smacked! I get nailed in the face!" (Roy, betrayed, frightened, surprised, describing shock and confusion at an [unbeknownst to him] prearranged dinner where he met his father for the first [and only] time in his life)

Although some of these phrases are not subtle, the emotional language used is. One must listen carefully for it: packed inside the phrases are a range of feelings that influenced the decision to run.

Language and word choice are not always clear-cut. Sociologist Thomas Scheff discusses the problems with locating "meaning, context, and interpretation" for microsociologists' studying emotion and describes issues with "ambiguity of expression":

There is basic ambiguity in language, even if we accept the simplifying myth that the meaning of a word is exactly defined by a dictionary. . . . Although we usually think that words and gestures have conventional and therefore fixed meanings, this is not quite the case. Conventional definitions of words serve only as an approximation of meaning in use. Human expression has an innovative character: conventional meanings may be modified or transformed. New words, gestures, and meanings may be invented on the spur of the moment to fulfill the expression that is needed. There is a creative element in human expression, as manifested in art and poetry, and in mundane settings such as spontaneously improvised metaphor, wit, and irony. (1990, pp. 38-39)

The young people in my sample did not exhibit an adult-style "emotional literacy" (Steiner, 1986, p. 97), but carefully listening and observing them during their storytelling revealed a hitherto unnoticed dimension of the runaway experience.[4] Emotion is located in more than words and verbal expression. Feelings are expressed in body posture, movement, facial expression, tone, and phrasing. In addition to important "made-up words" that runaways used when at a loss for more sophisticated emotional expression, their body movements and physical gestures revealed information about their emotional attitudes. Scheff explains that:

> another and much richer source of ambiguity is the manner of expression. The nonverbal components of utterance, the sounds (paralanguage) and the gestures (kinesics or body language), profoundly modify and enhance the linguistic meaning of expression. (1990, p. 38)

Mining this rich emotional information yields data concerning the contemporary adolescent runaway experience and the anger, hurt, fear, and betrayal that fuel it. I argue that by listening (and watching) closely to the runaways' stories, we learn much about how the young people felt about their relationships with their families, what they believed was important in their lives, and what they needed from adults to make a successful transition to adulthood.

I will show that using Hochschild's (1975, 1983) and Scheff's (1990) paradigms to study emotions is effective in uncovering important information about the runaway problem. Studying the emotional expressions and behaviors of runaways reveals the frame-work of the social bond. The emotion work and feeling rules that runaways used in deciphering their family struggles formed a picture of the social and emotional connections in families. Looking at the changes in the social bond—its a priori existence, its subsequent weakening or strengthening, its ruptures, its irreparability, and its reconnections—proves to be a useful way of "seeing" the effects of the resolution of the emotional crises. Runaways knew they "shouldn't" hate their mothers or siblings, but they felt anger and rage—enough to decide that the best resolution to some family crises was to go against the proscriptions and norms of the family—to run away.

PART I: FAMILY BONDS WEAKEN AND DISSOLVE

A weakening emotional connection in the family may lead to a youth's running away, or, as will be discussed later, may be repaired and healed in rapprochement. In this section, I will describe the hurt feelings, sadness, and anger that were reported by runaways who were experiencing a weakening of emotional attachment in their families: consequently, they leaned toward dissolving the alliance to the family norms and structures.

Hurt Feelings: "Mom Thinks I'm a Whore"

Hurt feelings were some of the common emotions that runaways reported experiencing when revealing what led them to run away from home. The underlying reason was often intense parental criticism. In girls' conflicts with their parents, accusations impugning sexual self-worthiness were characteristic.[5] Several of the girls in the sample expressed hurt, anger, and confusion over being called "whores" by their parents.

Princess was a fifteen-year-old adolescent with blonde curly hair falling around her shoulders. This white ninth grader had an eighteen-year-old boyfriend. The first time Princess ran away from home, she was eleven years old. She claimed to have run away from home "many" times; at the time of her interview, she had been gone about four weeks. Both her mother and stepfather were on disability at home. According to Princess, her mother had "some college" and she didn't know about her stepfather's level of educational attainment. Her stepfather was forty-three years old and her mother was thirty-five. She cited "fights with her mother" as her reason for running away and had no parental abuse—physical or sexual—to report. (She disclosed incestual abuse by another family member, but told me that she did not want to discuss it further.) Princess said that the fights with her mother ranged from "the color of socks that I'm wearing to major stuff" and described her life as a "continuous fight since I was eight years old." She said, "I'm not putting all the blame on her. I can start fights too, but most of the time, it's just because she's just trying to make my life miserable." Dressed in a large plaid shirt and jeans, she was articulate as she explained her disagreement with her mother's characterization of her behavior.

> Everything I do is wrong in my mother's eyes. She called me a prostitute because the place I was living when I ran away had men—one was thirty years old, one was twenty years old, and one was nineteen years old. . . . Because, like, it's a big drug house. Everyone around knows that, you know. . . . Anyway, so she says, "You're a prostitute!" and I said, "What do you mean?" She said, "Oh, you're not, are you? How do you pay for rent?" And I'm like, "Excuse me?" and she goes, "How do you pay for your rent? You sleep with a man for it!" And I'm like, "No, I'm sleeping with my boyfriend and that's it. I don't go sleeping with my best friend's boyfriend or my other best friend's boyfriend. No, I don't do that!" And then, it's just, like, . . .

Princess's voice trailed off in hurtful remembrance of her fights with her mother.

Stacey arrived at the shelter in shackles, arrested for an unarmed robbery charge. She was a sixteen-year-old white youth in tenth grade; she was from a rural region in western Massachusetts. Raised by her thirty-five-year-old single mother who worked in a hospital, "doing something about X rays," Stacey had one older sibling no longer at home whom she said "used to beat on me . . . when we were younger." She was fifteen years old when she first ran away and had been gone for two weeks this time—in Brooklyn, with her twenty-one-year-old boyfriend. She described "screaming fights" with her mother. Stacey said, "It's not like she's crazy, but sometimes . . . other people see it too; she's not all there—she has mood swings." Stacey continued:

> I could never sit down and tell my mom I got raped. I could never do something like that. She would never understand. She would laugh in my face and say, "Good! You had it coming to you!" The last time I tried to explain it to her, she laughed in my face! She was laughing at me! She thinks I'm a slut; she thinks I'm a hooker.

These girls had looks of disbelief on their faces as they recounted the hurtful words their mothers used against them. Teenage girls' issues of sexuality and gender are central to their sense of well-being and self-worth (Collins, 1991, p. 167; Chodorow, 1989, p. 47; Thompson, 1995; Leadbeater and Way, 1996; Pipher, 1994). That female runaways experienced further pain and anguish at having their parents characterize them in this manner was apparent.

Carmen, a Puerto Rican fourteen-year-old runaway from a low-income family, described coming home at 2:00 a.m. with "hickeys" on her neck and her mother calling her a *puta* (Spanish slang for *prostituta,* "prostitute"). The girl admitted that she had been out having sex with her boyfriend, but her mother's disrespectful characterization of her still hurt her feelings terribly. Carmen's age, the time of night she came home, and her activities are violations of social norms for fourteen-year-old girls, possibly middle- or upper-class-based norms, possibly ethnic and culturally based also. Her mother's characterization of her may be a signal from her mother that she is not the loving daughter that her mother expects her to be. Carmen, who interviewed in Spanish, told me her family is from "the Church" (*la Iglésia*). She said that if she got pregnant, she would "take it out" (*me lo quitaré*) and talked about getting in trouble with "the Church" for that. Her mother calling her names still hurt her, and possibly reminded her also of the religious norms she was violating.

The runaway girls' sadness revealed that these mother-daughter bonds were fraught with painful exchanges. However, runaways reported these events as more than conventional adolescent parent-daughter trauma, but as catalysts that eventually would lead the young girls to give up their struggles to sustain loving bonds and leave the family settings in despair and emotionally wounded. The mother-daughter connection eroded as hurt accumulated for these runaways. Sadness and rejection can lead to runaway behavior due to alienation from family connection; the runaways' hurt feelings led them to conclude that positive connections in their families were tenuous.

Brennan and colleagues describe the effect of alienation on runaways:

> Youth caught up in these processes may initially feel defeated and rejected. They may gradually acknowledge that they have nothing at stake in these institutions, and there may be a gradual emergence of the feeling that there is no reason to hold a commitment to the values, rules, or norms of these institutions. There may be a weakening of the feeling that he or she belongs to, or is part of, the family, the school, or the community. There is often nothing to gain but rejection and scapegoating by attempting to remain in these social arenas. There is little sense in being morally obligated to the rules, norms, or values of these institutions and even less reason to obey their strictures. (1978, p. 80)

Another kind of alienation from hurt feelings was located in outright rejection of the adolescent within the entire family structure.

Hurt Feelings: "Nobody Really Cares About Me"

Children yearn for, and thrive under, the acceptance, approval, and protection of their parents and the adults who raise and nurture them. Social theorists agree that to be emotionally, morally, and socially supported inside a loving family network is the preferred setting for the rocky uphill march toward adulthood that is contemporary American adolescence (Ianni, 1989, p. 55; Feldman and Gehring, 1990, p. 147; Demo, 1994, p. 307). But what about children who are "nobody's children"? How are they to handle feelings of rejection, insecurity, and fear? To which social structures can they maintain connections?

Many of the young people in my sample, as others have observed in runaways, did not want to run away. Indeed, they seemed to struggle *against* running away, preferring instead to try to remain socially attached through intact family bonds (Janus et al., 1987, p. 12). They expressed resentment and hurt feelings at the rupture of bonds between themselves and their parents. Although most runaways related that rage and anger precipitated their runs, beneath some angry accounts, a careful analysis revealed fear, hurt, and the pain of realizing that they lacked this most crucial social bond—love between parent and child.

Gregg was a skinny, lightweight, white male youth—he hadn't yet entered his "young man's" body at age thirteen, but claimed to really like the girls' attentions. He was a hip little guy with big baggy pants and a baseball cap turned backward. Gregg was on the run from his last foster home for three or four days before he was picked up and brought to the shelter. This eighth grader was from a rural town near the shelter. He said he had run away "many" times. The reason he cited for his current run was "too many rules at the foster home." He was not sure how old his mother was, but his father was thirty-four and his stepmother was forty years old. His father, a high school graduate, worked as a plumber, and his stepmother worked in an office. He didn't really know what to want for himself; he had no real hope of rapprochement with either of his parents because, as he put it, "Nobody really cares about me in my family":

> The only one who really cares about me is my older brother and his girlfriend—they're taking me in, hopefully. My Department of Social Services worker has to pull a few strings because they are kinda young. [His brother was nineteen years old.] I ran away from my last foster home. I stayed with some friends; I slept in someone's apartment I got in. I stay out of trouble. I didn't go to school.
>
> The foster home was awful. There was this real preppie kid I had to live with, and he was their own son and I couldn't stand him. I asked them to get me a new foster home, but they weren't doing it, so . . . I left. They were real jerks! I got grounded off of everything—for swearing, I got grounded off

of the phone for a week! They had two of their own kids, me, and two other foster kids.

When my dad and mom got divorced, I had to live with my dad, but he got remarried and my stepmother and him have two kids. She hates me! I can't stand her. She's the one that won't let me back there. I don't want to go back to her! She doesn't even like me. She hates me. I knew that she didn't like me. She didn't like me when she first saw me. It pisses me off. I almost punched her once. Cause she told me to get out of the room and I said, "No!" and I was with my little brother so I told her to fuck off and left.

My dad was never there. He worked all the time. My dad is always pissed! He's a plumber. He comes home and he sleeps, and when he wakes up, he's horrific pissed. I went to a foster home three or four months ago.

Gregg's story was fraught with grief and hurt: "the only one that really cares about me is my brother" showed how unloved he felt by his parents. He expressed his pain and his sense of unmet needs when he said, "My dad was never there," and "He comes home and he sleeps." Gregg's disappointment in his relationships with his family members was expressed in his perception that his stepmother did not love him.

Gregg's file read, "Bio mother abandoned him. Dad remarried. Dad and stepmom can't stand him." Gregg was trapped between families. The family that he was born into disintegrated and reformed into two new families, and neither parent wanted to be the primary custodial parent. Such circumstances are commonly documented in the literature of the sociology of the family.

One study indicated that almost one-third of American children will live for some period of time in a remarried household (Ahrons and Rodgers, 1994, p. 258). "Binuclear families" are families that have reformed after divorce, in which children from previous marriages now live with parents in separate households. These new family forms provide new challenges with which parents and young people have to struggle.[6] The emotional connection so critical between parents and children must remain firm for all family members to successfully survive divorces and consequent remarriages.

Many family theorists argue that it is not that families need to be "nuclear"; it is that they need to stay honest, close, open, and loving.[7] Young people especially need additional emotional support and the structure of a daily routine to withstand the crisis of a family rupture such as divorce (Furstenberg and Cherlin, 1994, p. 315).

Gregg, as he saw it, had thus far received neither emotional support nor a structured routine from any of his parents. Gregg's account was evidence of the devitalization of an emotional connection for this runaway and his family of origin, his reformed families through divorce, and his foster family. His search for allegiance and protection was fueled by sadness and hurt feelings.

Weakening of Sibling Bonds: Hurt and Anger

When the sibling bond is in disrepair, sometimes the relationship with a brother or sister is a source of unhappiness and anger for the runaway. Sometimes family scapegoating occurs (Brennan, Huizinga, and Elliott, 1978, p. 29). One child is designated as the "problem child" in the family, and the major share of negative emotion is heaped upon that child. One study participant reported resenting his baby sisters. Possibly the designated scapegoat in his family, he sneered with derision, saying, "I have younger sisters. They don't get in trouble—they're perfect" (Jesse).

Princess had trouble with her older brother, and she said she was afraid of him. An important potential familial alliance with her older brother was lost to this little sister:

> My mother has told me that I was a mistake—a total mistake! Ever since I was little, it was, "My older brother is the smart one; my brother's the best one; my brother's this; my brother's that!" I was scared of him—this was when I was really young. I was, like, scared of him for years. . . . You know, the last couple months before I was kicked out, we were starting to get a little bit close and hanging out and do stuff together. And then I got kicked out, and he hates me now; he totally hates me! He doesn't speak to me, and when he does, it's like, "Get the fuck out of the house!" . . . and everything, you know?

Princess expressed confusion over fear of her brother. His hatred of her mystified her. She could not fathom his fluctuating feelings toward her. As she puzzled over this, she revealed his rejection as a source of pain. She said this in a halting, pensive way, her voice cracking—"He totally hates me now . . . and everything, you know?" —her voice trailed off. Princess expressed her confusion and inability to understand and explain developments in the sibling relationship. Princess seems to suspect that her mother and brother have formed some kind of unspoken alliance against her at home—"I got kicked out and he hates me now"—wondering if the two events are connected. She felt she could not return home. "I could never go over to the house without feeling like I was going to die if I stayed one more minute!" she exclaimed. Her story points out how a weak sibling bond in disrepair contributes to the erosion of the overall family bond.

Weakened bonds in the family may presage a run. This theme was woven throughout the runaways' stories about hurt feelings and anger caused by insults and rejections from parents and siblings. By exploring hurt feelings and resentment, I have shown that sadness and rejection weaken bonds, loosening the adolescent's sense of obligation to comply to normative expectations in the family. If her mother calls her a whore, or his parents don't love him, or his mother insults his creativity and sense of self, then why stay? Why try? Why obey? These runaways began to question the worthiness of continuing to attempt emotional connection with their parents. When they reported hurtful or angry struggles with siblings, they were signaling the serious possibility of a rupture. Sibling dynamics play a key role in family harmony: sibling bonds have a profound emotional effect on adolescents. Paying attention to the fluidity of the bonds in families leads to explaining runaway behavior as one possible consequence of poor emotional connections in the family.

Studying social bonds in the family revealed family members' emotional connectedness and how well each member met the others' expectations. In the runaways' families, many adolescents reported feeling unloved and hurt, and more were furious. The overwhelming majority of runaways in this study expressed resentment, indignation, anger, and rage when they told the stories of their runs. They described family conflict—ranging from disagreement and argument over arbitrary rules to years of physical abuse and sexual assault. In the next section, I will show that, although the social bond can weather much confusion and conflict, it rarely survives outright destruction—caused by physical or sexual abuse (and both) and abandonment—that some participants relate experiencing.[8]

PART II: FAMILY BONDS RUPTURE

The social bonds that Hirschi describes are fluid, not static. Social connections can weaken when there is conflict and confusion among people. Composed of motivations such as attachment, belief, commitment, and involvement, bonds reflect the struggles over compliance with norms and expectations. These struggles represent emotional searches for belief and commitment; emotion also plays a central role in human attachment and involvement. When problems arise, social bonds weaken and can rupture. For adolescent teenagers in crisis, running away is one such emotional expression of a ruptured bond.

Although running away may appear as a single decisive act in a moment of crisis, it is an emotional process, often long in coming to fruition. The confusion that runaways experience is expressed in emotional struggles full of hurt and anger over obeying their parents and complying with their parents' expectations. When conditions such as physical and sexual abuse occur, the weak bond is abandoned.

The following accounts of running away illuminate the emotional motivation behind the decision to run, as well as the confusion involved when young people make decisions to leave the family setting.

Anger Over Physical Abuse

Teenagers often consider running away as the best solution to family struggles, especially when chronic and acute physical and/or sexual abuse by parents has occurred. Given that the social bond is held in place by elements such as attachment, commitment, involvement, and belief, it is difficult to picture all of those elements being nurtured and encouraged by the nonnormative treatment of abusive parents. In the following accounts, runaways reported acts that give a painfully clear image of what severe physical/sexual abuse looks and feels like to an adolescent victim. Anger, fear, and confusion motivate these abused teens to run away. The ruptured social bond is evident in these accounts.

One young Latina from a nearby city shared the rage she felt toward her father that caused her to flee her family's home. Isabel, a tiny, fourteen-year-old of Caribbean heritage, wearing Cleopatra eye makeup, sat with her legs crossed at the knees and each hand gripping the chair's arm rests. She spoke intently, using a forced, resentful tone, and looked worried. Her file contained the note, "Very Abusive Father," and this was her story:

> To me, my father could die. One time I came home late and my father started yelling. I started crying and my mom started arguing and I locked myself in my room. Then my father came in and started arguing and all this and I started crying. I got down on my knees and just told my mom, I said, "I swear to God I'll kill him if I have to hurt him back! I swear to God I'll kill him!" My father tried to hurt me and my mom tried to hold him back! I went and got some things and my mom agreed with me staying at my best friend's house . . .
>
> A father should be trustable. In my house, when I come home, I get yelled at—first thing I do when I walk in the door! I used to slam the door in his face, I used to swear at him—I didn't care! See, when I was pregnant, my dad got drunk and came home and started hitting me. And I was pregnant and he tried to throw me down the stairs! . . . To me, I don't care—to me, my father could die and I don't care! I'm not going to feel sorry for him. Is he going to feel sorry for me? The problems I'm having now—they tell me that I'm taking it out on other people. My mom is dying, and my father losing the baby, and all these things in court now. . . . I'm on probation for assault and battery . . .

When Isabel used a weapon and beat a girl at her school, she was charged with assault and battery. She was at the shelter because she had violated her probation. Her file recorded her disturbing history with allusions to incidents of early sexual abuse, suicide attempts, her gang affiliation, her use of "beer, pot, and smoking cocaine," and three previous runs—two from foster home placements. She had three brothers who lived at home; she never mentioned them in the interview. The file also noted, "Her father pushed her down the stairs when she was pregnant, causing a miscarriage."

In her account of this incident, she said, "I don't care!" while she seemed to care very much—in fact she seemed to care enough to wish he were dead. Isabel was "crying" during this fight and holding herself back from "hurting her father back." She seemed to be in a rage as she told the story. Isabel says, "a father should be trustable," indicating a cognitive struggle and an emotional disappointment with the expectations she has for a family life and the way things actually are in her family. This child struggled with familial expectations. To "not care" about a parent is letting go of an expectation that a loving relationship should exist between parent and child. Young people want to love, and be loved by, their parents. Physical confrontations with her father created an emotional trauma for Isabel. Her resolution was to get away from that house and the abusive parent.

Anger, fear, and disappointment were her responses. These feelings fueled her decision to get out of that house and to go stay with her (twenty-year-old) best friend Evelyn. She described Evelyn as a friend of her mom's. Isabel stressed the importance of her long talks about life and feelings with her older friend, and how much fun she had with Evelyn when they did things together, such as cleaning house and going shopping at the mall. Evelyn was Puerto Rican and they spoke Spanish when they were together:

> Evelyn could be a counselor—she sits down and talks to me. We talk, for like three hours—about our problems, like the time she was yelling. And the kind of problems she has and that it is the same thing I am going through. She looks at me and it reminds her of when she was a little kid. That the same thing I am going through, she went through.

The authenticity of Evelyn's interest in Isabel, coupled with sharing of experience and that Evelyn "sits down and talks to me," made Evelyn an alluring companion for Isabel. This runaway felt safe and protected in the connection with her friend, in stark opposition to the physical and verbal abuse she experienced from her father. As one social bond—the paternal connection in the family—dissolved, another—connecting her to a peer community—flourished.[9]

Betrayal and Violation: "Too-Strict Mom"

Not all children run away from home because of physical and sexual abuse. Others run because they believe their parents are overprotective, meddling, or nonnegotiating. Are these children simply unruly and disobedient? A common expectation in many traditional families is that parents make the rules in the house and the children obey, or make counterdemands, and a negotiation of sorts takes place. As discussed more fully in Chapter 1, modern middle-class families tend to implement authority in flexible and loving ways, with variations due to religion, socioeconomic background, race and ethnicity, educational levels, and other such factors. However, many runaways at the shelter reported that the rules in their families were simply too strict and unreasonable, and they felt they weren't given much chance at negotiations. They resented not having any voice in the making of the rules and reported that they outright disobeyed their parents' rules. They complained of not being able to talk to their parents, of not feeling heard. Several young people told angry stories about having their privacy violated, being mistrusted, ordered around, disbelieved, or treated unfairly in general.

Amy told a story of the shame and embarrassment she felt after her mother made public revelations of entries from her diary. Her mother and sister lived at home. Her mother worked as a convenience store clerk to support the two children. She ran away for the first time a month before she came to the shelter. A tall, blonde fourteen-year-old, she never stopped squirming and wiggling as she rattled on nonstop—shocked, surprised, and indignant about what her mother had done to her. Her mother located Amy's bag and searched through her daughter's belongings, finding a diary:

> My boyfriend is eighteen years old, and I like my boyfriend a lot, and she thinks my boyfriend is really bad. I was fighting with my mom for awhile and she went through all my stuff and read my diary. And there's stuff about me and my boyfriend in

it and . . . see, it says, like, what I've done with my boyfriend in it. Like anything that I've done with my boyfriend and how long we've been going out and stuff, and now they're gonna use that shit to put statutory rape charges on my boyfriend.[10] We got in a fight, and I told her, "I'm not going to be home when you get home!" . . . So I called my boyfriend and he came and got me and we spent the night in a hotel. . . . But I got caught 'cause I went to school on Monday morning and they caught me there.

I'm upset with her because she's gonna put statutory rape charges on my boyfriend and he's gonna go to jail! There's no way he can avoid it—maybe not show up in court—but if she puts statutory rape charges on him, he's going to go to jail, and that is extremely pissing me off!

I feel extremely raided—it feels like they took everything that was ever mine and took it away from me—it's wrong! Other than that, things like that . . . things that it says in my diary, and she found a letter that I wrote to him and they made copies of it all!

Amy's mother went through Amy's things and took her diary, read it, made copies, and shared it with social service agencies and police officers and legal personnel. At the time that Amy was in the shelter, both she and her boyfriend had been arrested for being in possession of a stolen vehicle, but Amy was not as concerned with the upcoming criminal charges against her as she was worried and obsessed with the notion of her boyfriend "doing time for statutory rape charges." She was mortified and embarrassed at the idea of copies of pages from her diary circulating and felt violated ("extremely raided") that her mother not only searched through her diary and read it but then shared the details of Amy's intimate life with lawyers, social workers, and police agents. The sense of betrayal and violation led Amy to run away from her mother; Amy preferred to be with her boyfriend.

Amy also disclosed that between the ages of five to nine years old, she lived with an abusive stepfather who "beat the crap out of me and stuff." She said that her five-year-old sister back at home was "like my best friend 'cause my mom was having really bad custody battles and I would take care of her." Amy cited her reason for running away as being "because I don't want to be with my mom":

> I ran away from home because I have a lot of problems with my mom; we fight a lot. And we get in physical fights and I don't hit her because she's my mom, but . . . she . . . 'cause I respect her for that, 'cause she's my mom, but she just . . . we have really different viewpoints.
>
> I have to be in when it gets dark out. I have to be in by like 5:30 p.m.—I have to be in my house and I'm not allowed to go out! It's like—it's not fair! And I'm not allowed to get phone calls past 8:30 p.m., you know? It's like, it sucks! She's extremely paranoid. I'm not allowed to see my boyfriend because she just won't let me, and if I go out with somebody, she basically has to give approval.

The familial bond with her mother was in a ruptured state, while the peer connection with her boyfriend solidified.

The social bond with a parent weakens when runaway youths feel betrayed or violated. Runaways reported in their stories the fear, hurt, and surprise they felt upon discovering that parents had read their diaries and betrayed their secrets.[11] These conditions often provoked adolescents to run away. Jean's situation with her guardian was one such case. She concluded that "she's just not ready for parents" because she felt that what they did was meddle and give unsolicited advice:[12]

> What gets me is that she works with all kinds of people at a restaurant downtown, right? And when I call up, they are all giving me lectures about how to be, right? "Excuse me, you aren't my father; you aren't even my friend, so just stay out of it!" I just hang up on them. It bugs the hell out of me; she tells everyone in the place everything that ever happened to me. Bugs the crap out of me! I have a diary, and I write in it, and I come home and she's reading my diary! I call the restaurant, and everyone is in there, like, lecturing me about my life! I told her one thing about this guy, and she has her boyfriend come and give me a lecture about sex! I told him, "Get the

fuck out of my face! Excuse me, but you are nothing to me—nothing!" I'm just not ready for parents!

Jean expressed a confusion of anger, embarrassment, and irritation—"Bugs the crap out of me!"—she said in exasperation. She was indignant that strangers at her aunt's job at the restaurant were talking about her behind her back, discussing even her sex life. She couldn't telephone her aunt without a co-worker coming onto the telephone to give Jean opinions that Jean did not want. This angered Jean and caused her to yell at her aunt's co-worker: "You are nothing to me!" It was clear that Jean needed privacy and respect for her life and her belongings. She was not experiencing the loving guidance and nurturing that her mother could be giving her in a way that she felt she deserved. Instead, she felt betrayed and invaded by her aunt's attempts to parent her.

The emotional bond that connects parents and children weakens and can rupture when runaways perceive parents as disrespectful. Furthermore, when parents invade the privacy of their teenage children, feelings of betrayal and violation run high; this can spur runaways to leave home.

PART III: IRREPARABLE BONDS

Ruptures in the family bond become irreparable under three conditions: if the parents abuse the child so severely that any rapprochement seems impossible; if the parents abandon the child and it is impossible for them to ever locate one another; and in the event of parental death or if the child commits suicide. Some of the stories that runaways shared about the events in their lives appeared to represent the dissolution of possibilities of them ever reuniting with their families of origin.

Who Can an Abandoned Child Trust?
"Throwaway/Pushout" Runaways

For some families, the healing of a ruptured social bond probably will never be possible. Isaiah's story was one such tragic case. Isaiah was a big fifteen-year-old, born in Alabama to African-American parents. He was the only participant in my study who had no chance at any kind of rapprochement with his family because he was a youth for whom federal agencies have developed the term "pushout" or "throwaway" child. Isaiah's mother abandoned him, as he revealed in this story:

> We were living in a motel outside of town and my mom ran away. I was in the shower one day, and I had left my money and my cigarettes under the mattress. She calls out, "Isaiah, I'm going to the store; I'll be right back!" And I thought, "She don't have any money—why she going to the store? She wouldn't buy me a candy bar!" So I ran out of the bathroom and looked under the mattress, and my cigarettes and my money were gone! I ran outside and she just got in the car and left, and I haven't seen her since!
>
> . . . I mean, I should be home right now; I should be—what time is it? My mom should be serving me dinner or doing our laundry, me and my brothers, but NO, NO, NO—I'm home. I'm doing my laundry in somebody else's house, and she's out doing her thing, and I'm acting like I'm the mother!

Isaiah sat forward with both hands on his knees as he told this story—sad, amazed, and hurt. "I haven't seen her since!" expressed his surprise and dismay. Isaiah seemed to be slowly realizing the depth of his predicament. "My mom should be serving me dinner" revealed an expectation of family behavior, and the depth of his disappointment and loss was expressed by "but NO, NO, NO." Isaiah described what he thought and feared would happen to him next:

> Well, OK, when I go to court, sometimes, and the judge probably gives me a good thing. She'll send me out to a place like this. I'll go to school; I'll be class president—honors, everything. Everything you can name, and they just snatch it away from me. I mean, it's like if they let me sniff a piece of pizza, and then I'll start to bite it . . . and then—they just, "ssssst!" Take it away, like, "psy-y-y-ch . . . "

But these intense and eloquent expressions of mistrust and despondency belie the salient features about Isaiah: his general likeableness and sense of humor. Isaiah was very easygoing: he quickly made friends with peers and staff alike. Such "people-pleasing" is a characteristic survival tool of some runaways and homeless youths. People-pleasing describes the ability to manipulate social bonding to ensure positive and friendly connection in order to meet the needs of the "people-pleaser" for protection and attachment (Butler, 1991, p. 33).

Irreparable social bonds with parents develop when parents disappear or die, precluding any chance of repair. In 1990, over 125,000 abandoned children were in the United States (Finkelhor, Hotaling, and Sedlak, 1990). The suffering represented in these figures is difficult to conceptualize. Many of these thrown-away/pushed-out/abandoned children cycle through the runaway system in foster families, group homes, and juvenile placement facilities until they turn eighteen, which by no means guarantees an end to adolescent misery or their safe and healthy transition to adulthood. The scars of unrepaired bonds can linger throughout an entire lifetime. But at least abandoned runaways have a chance to heal. In the next section, runaways share thoughts about suicide—the ultimate irreparable bond—and discuss the hopeless situation surrounding thoughts of ending their lives altogether.

Bonded to No One: Suicide

The search for connection can get very confusing for runaways. At times, it seemed some runaways were left hanging in limbo. Another pattern in emotional bonding can be seen when they discussed moments of feeling disconnected altogether—unable to emotionally attach in their families, with their friends, to the police, or with a counselor. Some even discussed suicide attempts, reflecting a final, permanent, literal disconnection.

Roy ran away from his last group home placement because they were too strict:

> I've been in foster care for four years straight. Different places. Two years I was off and on at different foster homes. I couldn't handle it, so I'd run away.

Roy recounted an entire elaborate, albeit misguided, plan to latch onto somebody, somewhere, but to no avail. On the run from the juvenile facility, he "caused trouble somewhere" to get picked up by police and get some protection from the street. He then lied to the police about the nature of the trouble at the group home (he falsely accused someone of threatening his life) to ensure a new social service placement. Roy was at the shelter awaiting a county court disposition for a different juvenile facility placement. Several bonds dissolved at once for this youth, and no people came forward with whom he felt he could place his allegiance. His problems with his mother fed his confusion and feelings of disconnection. His expectations of a happy family life and peaceful foster care were disappointed. Even the ability to trust in a fair system of justice was weakened by his own dishonesty in dealing with the police.

Another boy told of how he ran away from his mother's side in the parking lot of the county courthouse on the way to his hearing because he was afraid of "being sent away by the court." Jesse was one participant who stood out because of his monosyllabic replies and complete lack of affect. His files contained the entry "possible sexual abuse." Janus and colleagues (1987) describe characteristic responses of males to sexual abuse as, among other symptoms, "long periods of silence, persistent loss of self-confidence and self-esteem, attitude of self-blame, marked irritability, sudden onsets of phobic reactions, a fear of being alone," and more (p. 62). Jesse sat staring away from me through the entire interview. He answered in inaudible monosyllabic words or short phrases. His voice had a snide lilt—a kind of sing-song sarcastic tone, "Yea-ea-eah?" It occurred to me during the interview that something was wrong, that he was furious and shut down at the same time. "Physically aggressive toward smaller children," "stubborn," has "severe asthma," and "hates his stepfather—wants to see his mom and stepfather break up," were all notations recorded in his files.

Jesse was twelve years old and came from a nearby rural town. His family was white working class (his mother worked in a nursing home and his father worked in a electronic parts factory). He had little sisters who lived at home—he reported feeling some antagonism toward them. Later I found out that the staff had to restrain him several times for attacking other residents at the shelter. According to this noncommunicative and inarticulate offender, neither the family system nor the legal community were perceived as safe havens for his trust and attempts at connection. Fear motivated him to bolt. However, he had no where to go from there. He returned home later that night.

Several runaways in my sample mentioned suicide attempts as a low point in their struggles to resolve crises of trust and meet their needs for approval and attachment. In the disconnection and de-vitalization of their social bonds with family, friends, and community service workers, suicide becomes the ultimate means of discon-nection for runaways:

> If I didn't have pot to smoke, I'd have to kill myself—how else would I deal with all this shit? (Stacey)

> I was so mad when my mother's boyfriend raped me that I tried to kill myself. (Chabela)

In the same vein, Gregg's suicide attempt illuminated his desper-ate loss of anyone with whom to bond. Luckily, he had "a lot of female friends" to whom he talked about the important issues in his life. The emotional connection of the social bond with his peers was literally saving Gregg's young life:

> I went to a foster home three or four months ago. I feel much better because I was mad, and I almost killed myself a couple weeks ago, actually a week ago, 'cause I was so depressed—but all my friends tell me to hang in there because I'll be fine.

Constituting a national public health crisis, 22 percent of run-away youths in shelters report attempts at suicide (NASW, 1993). The mistreatment of runaway teenagers by parents, police, and social service agencies, however concerned or well-intentioned, worsens the problem of runaway teens. The tragic high rates of adolescent runaway suicide attempts brings an immediacy to bear in the need to solve this problem.

PART IV: REPARATION OF BONDS:
LONGING FOR PROTECTION AND RECOGNITION

Running away from home did not necessarily have a sad ending. Except in cases of extreme abuse, abandonment, or death, runaways shared accounts of change, healing, and a fluidity in their emotional connections that led to repairing the ruptures among family members, making possible a vision of hope for the future for runaways and their families. Their accounts of repairing and rapprochement also revealed runaways' ability, desire, and preference for emotional well-being in the family.

Some bonds were damaged beyond repair. Several runaways reported severe and chronic levels of physical torture and incestuous rape in their families: it is doubtful whether those family bonds could heal.[13] In some such cases, feelings of anger and fear calmed as runaways found places of connection and social attachment with people other than their parents—with siblings, friends, schoolmates, and foster families. These runaways also told stories of feeling love for, and close connection to, community workers such as the staff at the shelter.

Other runaways rendered accounts of healing and reconnection in the family. Although all study participants had negative stories of the bonds in their families withering and being destroyed, the revitalization and repair in relationships with family members revealed in some of the runaways' accounts were inspiring. Whether the reconnections occurred between sister and brother, father and son, stepparent and child, or among other runaways and staff members at the shelter, the desire of the adolescent to be in healthy bonded connection to other people, and the resilient nature of the emotional connection, was apparent.

In this section, I outline the dynamic nature of the changes in emotional connections of the social bond for the runaways. Although running away from home created a break of the family social bond, many of the runaways described situations in which emotional connectedness was dynamic and shifting—it weakened, then may have repaired, or strengthened. Examining the emotional interactions in the runaways' stories of their healing among their peers, in school, and with people in the wider community with whom they interact—police and social workers—provided observations of the fluid nature of the bond. The stories highlighted the important factor that not all runaway situations are hopeless and irreparable. The emotional connectedness that the young people so desperately seek can be repaired and strengthened, as some of these testimonies will show.

Crises of Trust in Peer Bonds: Belonging and Rejection

The fluidity of social connectedness for the runaways was apparent in their accounts of interactions with peers. When the bond with their families weakened or ruptured, runaways reported that they often turned to their peers for support, validation, protection, and emotional connection. However, they also reported that such peer connections seem tenuous. At times, runaways could find emotional connection with friends; at other times, they felt rejected by, or rejecting of, their friends.

Although the runaway was running away from home and the family, not school, or peers, or community organizations per se, peer groups play a key role in adolescent decision making and development:

> What we concluded after years of observing and interviewing in three communities is that peer groups are the primary means by which teenagers share and validate personal and social growth as they expand their everyday experience into the community beyond the family. (Ianni, 1989, p. 50)

Feelings about peers are intense and important for the troubled youths in my sample, and central to the runaway experience. First of all, peer relationships are the arena in which runaways sort out issues of identity—what it means to be a teenager. Several runaways spontaneously supplied detailed descriptions of how they rank and categorize one another:

> It's tough; it's tough being a teenager now 'cause you got so much out there. So many different roads, and you don't know the good ones from the bad ones. 'Cause they all look good,

you know. You go out there, and you got the glamour of being a jock, or the popularity of being the team captain, or the person with the most bowls, or whatever, and that looks great! Or you can go out and get stoned at a party and everybody thinks you're cool now 'cause you went out and got stoned. Everybody thinks you're cool now, 'cause you got ten baskets in basketball. . . . And there's even—everything looks good; it's hard to know which ones are the bad ones and the good ones. (Eric)

I've met plenty of sixteen-year-old girls and they think I'm involved in the Department of Social Services to make me popular! I'm not in the DSS system to make me popular, but to really get somewhere in my life. They think they're going to make themselves "Joe Cool" and they think they can do this cause they're in DSS! They're all looking "bad," and they're all in trouble and these problems, and make themselves out to be a different person from who they really are.

It's definitely, "The tougher you are, the badder you are." In your high school, there are people who are popular because they're on the basketball team. But the people who do drugs are usually more popular because they do this stuff. The ones that got in trouble with the police are the more popular people. The other ones are usually preppie and they got the expensive clothes and they think that just because they paid $80 to have their hair done makes them the most gorgeous persons in the whole world. The people I hang out with are my true friends because they don't try to make me out to be somebody else, and I don't see why I should have to play myself to be anybody. I should be able to play myself to be me and nobody else. (Anne)

Parents, social workers, teachers, police agents, community workers, and other adults who work with youths might underestimate and discount the importance of peer influence in decision making and meaning construction for adolescents. I contend that this key aspect of adolescent life should be highlighted. In fact, peer influence is a contributing factor to combating the adolescent alienation that leads to runaway behaviors. Young people spend time with one another, interacting, teaching one another, and learning from one another as part of their transition to adulthood—a survival mechanism that is essential to their healthy maturation. They spend time together to purposely distinguish themselves from adults. Peer interaction is not elective behavior for young adults: it is crucial for their individuation from parents and family and for the evolution of their notions of self-esteem and feelings of self-worth. Ianni describes one aspect of the importance of "peer sharing" as "representing a new way of relating without the hierarchical controls of parents or the parent-constrained relationships with siblings" (1989, p. 36). Whether teens hang out in "gangs, cliques, or crews," peer interaction is fundamental and necessary to the genesis of "reputation, recognition, and the development of an identity" (Ianni, 1989, p. 26).

Although a confusing struggle in the family may lead a youth to choose to run, he or she may also respond to a pull from positive formations in the socioemotional bonds among peers as well. This pull to be with peers instead of at school or at home is strong for runaways, in part because the family bond has eroded and because the peer bond evolves into a source of acceptance and protection. In effect, in the absence of their own family support, runaways sought to be "adopted" by their friends. The combination for an adolescent of being unhappy at home and feeling that her family is maltreating her and having positive and strong associations among her peer groups can lead to runaway behavior (Brennan, Huizinga, and Elliott, 1978, p. 273). This was the case with Carmen, a Latina who was caught up in getting attention from "the boys." She describes her struggle to try to get to school:

> When I turned twelve years old, really about eleven, I began to run around with many people who used drugs, and stole things out of stores. I began to quit school, I began to smoke cigarettes and pot, and I went to the dances, looking for boys—the ones to buy the pot, the ones to smoke pot with and go out with. I was living in Dinwiddie Flats. I went to the park where all the boys from Bellhurst—we would go there to get high. . . . And I began to steal also, and I got caught, and I went to court. I got probation; I began to steal and come home at 2:00 a.m. Sometimes I would stay home, but I usually would hit the streets with the boys.

I quit going to school; it's like something came over me—the boys would beg me not to go to school and I would say, "OK," and not go! It's that—the boys from the Flats, we'd be walking around—me, my girlfriend, well, it's my sister, but it's like we're girlfriends, and another girlfriend, and the boys would say, "Oooh baby, you look so good, come and play with us," and they would treat us good . . .

Fourteen-year-old Carmen described her father as "sixty-something years old," her mother as a foster mother ("there's so many in the house"), and complained that she was supposed to be indoors by 7:00 p.m. She was not sure how many brothers and sisters she has; some are back in the Caribbean Islands. She expressed feeling alienated, distant, uninterested in the goings-on in her family, and fascinated and appreciated among her peers in the neighborhood. "Something comes over her" and she was pulled toward her connections with her friends. Carmen's biggest "problem" seemed to be that she was sexually precocious, and wanted to play around, have fun, and not obey her mother or go to school. For Carmen, the emotional pull of her peer friendships was much stronger than a need for bonding with family or school.[14]

The adolescents formed close intimacies quickly in the shelter. There was an emotional immediacy to life on the run. They never knew when they would see one another again. An oft-repeated account was one in which a youth went to school one morning, and upon returning from school that day, found that his or her roommate had run away—never to be seen again. The impermanence and constant shuffling of the youths through system placements, and because of their own running away, caused runaways to be thrown together and wrenched apart at a moment's notice. But instead of deadening them—numbing their feelings, or causing them to put up "emotional walls" against seeking passionate connections with one another—it seemed to make them redouble their efforts to connect and reconnect somewhere. Runaways continually attempted rapprochement at home with family, with other friends, or in the community service agencies to which they were assigned. Their efforts were testaments to the resiliency of the social bond.

Runaways shared accounts about their decisions to run from conflicts with their parents, which included the influence of being drawn to one another. However, due to the dialectical nature of social bonds, devitalization also occurred in emotional relationships among peers. One sad female runaway had so many problems with the other youths making fun of her at school that she quit going there, "for right now":

> I've been going to school, but I've been having a lot of problems at East High. They read in the paper about how my mom beat me up, and they think it's a big joke, and it just makes me feel even worse. So I stopped going for awhile. I got in a fight one day with this girl in my school, and it doesn't really have anything to do with my family or anything, but I just give up. It's too close to my family right now. (Gretchen)

The ridicule of her peers was too much, and she felt ashamed and embarrassed to go back to school. Painful humiliation was too difficult to bear for an already emotionally shaky young girl who had run away from an abusive situation at home. She knew she needed either the nurturing support of her peers or to not be around them at all.

The following account came from a female runaway who felt alienated from her mother. She felt that her boyfriend was her best friend and she could "talk to him about anything." Her mom tried to break them up, but Princess insisted that he was a good influence on her:

> He tried to get me to stay in school and my mom would say, "Yeah, he probably influenced you not to go to school!" and all this stuff. I said, "Look, he actually tried to get me to go to school!" and all that. He'd wake me up every morning and tell me, "It's time to go to school!" And I'd be like, "No, I'm too tired, I don't want to sit through class and be stressed out all day!" But now that I'm finally set that I want my GED, he's like, "It's OK. I'll help you out; I'll support you," and all that . . .

Princess experienced her boyfriend as a caring friend who tried to help make her life work for her. Her mother thought that Princess's boyfriend was a no-good scoundrel. Princess tried to explain to her mother that her boyfriend woke her up to go to school and that it was she—Princess—who was always ditching school. She resented having to explain this to her mother, who believed that Princess's boyfriend was preventing her from going to school. Princess was exasperated with her mother. Princess thought the reason her mother was so vigilant about her sex life, her boyfriends, and her sexuality related to the stories that Princess was told about her mother's adolescence:

> I don't know. I think my mom's really afraid of me growing up to be like her, because when she was sixteen, she was kicked out of her house and she had a bad situation. She's afraid I'm gonna be like that. She was abused at home, sexually and physically abused at home. She became a prostitute and had my brother. She got out of that, had me. She was an alcoholic.

For differing reasons, runaways reported that adults often discounted the support given to them by peers; to the runaways, some adults seemed to refuse to acknowledge the importance of the emotional connections that formed among young people. Adolescence is a time of transition from childhood to independence and adulthood. In accounts similar to Princess's, runaways reported that adults often ignored or discounted emotional and social connections with peers, which could be seen as essential to teens' moral development and social well-being.

Runaways and Schools:
"Ditching to Chill with Friends"

The roles played by, and conditions in, the educational institutions in the United States are changing. The most salient purpose of schools for adolescents in America is to prepare them with the technical and cultural skills necessary to make the successful transition from the role of child/student to the role of adult/worker. The educational system has also widened its purpose to include socialization in more personal areas, such as teaching youth citizenship, pertinent healthy and hygienic behavior, sex and drug education—in short, providing training formerly offered within the family structure (Feldman and Elliott, 1990).

Several conditions give schools a prominent place in the lives of contemporary teens. First, since the turn of the century in the United States, when compulsory national public education was extended to include high school, adolescents are supposed to remain in school until eighteen years of age. Second, access to college has widened to include social classes other than those youths solely from the upper echelon. Moreover, the school day has been extended, resulting in teenagers spending a great many hours per day in this particular social arena. Although in comparison to other countries American schools are shown to be academically dismal, they have gradually improved in the latter half of this century (Feldman and Elliott, 1990). The numbers of teens completing high school has increased (Ianni, 1989, p. 104). However, accessibility to, and participation in, the educational facilities is uneven across racial, ethnic, and socioeconomic class divisions (MacLeod, 1987, p. 97).[15] Any problems with educational structures are further magnified for young people from troubled families.

Although some runaways utilized educational institutions as places to experience much-needed routine and regularity in an otherwise chaotic personal situation, unfortunately (but not surprisingly), the overwhelming majority expressed strong negative emotions toward their affiliations with schools. Three runaways reported quitting junior high school over math, and one girl said her father "used to beat her" because she would flunk her math tests. These youths reported that they "ditched school to be with friends" and "prefer to chill out with friends." Many had their own strategies for attendance:

I don't go to school every day. I'll go to school the whole week; I'll go to school half a week; I'll miss a day, then I'll go to school the rest of the week. Then I'll go to school a whole day. I miss about two or three days a month because I just—I hate going five days a week—two days of weekend! It just gets boring, and every once in a while I need a break. I tell my mom I'm going to school; I walk somewhere. I don't go to school—I just chill. I go to other people's houses—most of them have already quit! (Jimmy)

Jimmy was a fourteen-year-old white youth from a family of four—his mother and two other siblings. His mother worked in a nursing home; his ex-stepfather physically abused him. Jimmy was placed out of his house because the social worker had deemed the family setting as unacceptable: the rented apartment was in disrepair and no furniture was provided. Jimmy had been on the run for five days from his foster family placement, where "they just made me their slave." Jimmy seemed more concerned with having autonomy at school (and at home) than in actually getting an education or connecting with peers at school. The youths' comments continue:

> I go to school but I don't understand. I go to Westside for seven years and they teach different. I can't do fractions. I can only do multiplication tables. I was good in sixth grade and seventh grade, and then I came up here and they were doing algebra and stuff like that, and I don't know how, so I quit. (Chabela)

> So he put assault and battery charges against me at that school, and I went to Juvenile. At Juvenile, they got books, they set you up, like, algebra and that's the pits. Every year they switch off between sciences and between a social studies thing and an art thing. See, my learning ability or my level is, actually, I can do twelfth grade work in English, history, science. My math is good—I can do geometry! Juvy didn't have any geometry! They gave me basic English for eleventh grade. I'd be into more academic—I don't care! But not basic! They're like, you're in here or you're out in six months! But still give me work I can do! I'd be sitting in the back of the classroom, scribbling on piece of paper because I'll have my homework assignment done ten minutes before class is even over! And the teacher would ask, "What are you doing?" And I'd say, "Yeah, well my assignment's done!" I did it all and she'd give me another assignment—and boom! I did it within the next ten minutes of class! (Roy)

Roy was a sixteen-year-old white youth from a nearby city who had a child with a previous girlfriend. He had three siblings and came from a working-class family: his mother worked a menial job in a hospital, his father was a truckdriver, and his stepfather worked at the telephone company. He first ran away when he was twelve years old; he had run many times and hadn't lived at home since he was thirteen years old because of physical abuse. He talked at length about his plans to get a GED and about how to get into a nearby community college. Roy was awaiting placement in a local independent living program—a rare opportunity for older runaway teens. His social workers were hoping he would be able to handle it since he had just successfully completed a program at a secured facility in Hartford.[16]

Some youths reported feeling bored, frustrated, and humiliated by interactions with teachers that demonstrate their lack of skills and ineptitude at school: "I don't know how, so I quit!" Troubled youths primarily sought people with whom to make emotional connections. They did not see "studying math" as an essential or urgent need. Junior and high schools could have been positive arenas in which to anchor America's troubled adolescents. However, runaways reported that they sought approval, validation, self-worth, and connection elsewhere, usually hanging out among their friends.

The problem for these youths was twofold. First, they did not experience the offerings at educational institutions as relevant or compelling because, for differing reasons, they did not perceive the teachers or curricula as meeting their interests or needs. Second, rather than being interested in "an education" per se, as it was being presented to them, runaways seemed more preoccupied with emotional struggles in their families and their need to find emotional and social connections.[17] MacLeod (1987) discusses complexities of the educational system from the viewpoint of socioeconomic status and how the "curriculum should meet the needs and concerns of working-class kids" (p. 154). Examining runaway behavior and its relation to the school system led me to focus on the relationship between family conflict and the influence of emotional trauma on an adolescents' ability to garner from their educational institutions—and the personnel in them—the support, validation, and connection that is available to runaways at school. Some youths stayed in school while on the run; some had dropped out long before they ran away from home. Their reports conflicted, and there was internal variation in their opinions about school: there was no clear message that they "all hated school," although I did get the sense that services for runaways' needs could be improved in the educational system. Runaways continued to search outside of educational institutions to have their emotional and social needs met.

Emotional Connections: "Circling the Wagons" Against Community Interventions

Another important pattern of emotional bonding that became evident from runaways' stories was the forming and fluctuating of bonds with people in the runaways' families and with community personnel such as police, social workers, and counselors. These emotional connections often shifted in unexpected directions. Some runaways felt protective toward their families and closed ranks in a "them against us" formation to ward off social workers and Department of Social Services agents.[18] Young people reported feeling increased allegiance toward parental connections rather than with the larger protective community, as social bonds fell apart through ineffectual connections with social workers whom they viewed as intrusive. Or the opposite occurred: runaways sought protection from a school psychologist or the parent of a friend, as the acceptance and love failed them in their own family. Like swinging rung to rung on a playground gym, runaway teenagers reached for the next firm support to fulfill their need to stay socially connected.

One young girl told of being on a run and crashing in a crack house. Eva was a white fifteen-year-old who was very interested in boys. She was thirteen years old when she first ran away and had run approximately six times; this present run had lasted five weeks. She ran away from home because of physical abuse by her alcoholic mother. She was from the rural part of a New England state and was in a city when the events in her story occurred. Staying at the drug-plagued apartment was not going well for Eva. In the middle of her story, she casually mentioned that:

> the Department of Social Services and the police weren't really looking for me while I was out. I was reported and everything, but. . . . They took four days just to get my CHINS warrant out. I had gone down to the police station to turn in this guy for raping me and . . . they pulled out my CHINS

warrant, so my parents came down and got me. I went back to my house, and [laugh] I wasn't there for very long. I was there for a few days before Easter, until a few days after school ended, and then I ran away again.

This girl must have been terrified while with her peers in this chaotic and dangerous setting at the crack house, which she described as "a really cruddy apartment with a sleazy landlord." Her peer group proving to be ineffectual in affording protection, she sought assistance from a community source—in this instance, the police. She might have known that the police would discover she was a truant and a runaway, arrest her, and remand her to the custody of her family. Maybe she hoped they would. Even though she earlier had fled her parents' home, Eva was guided by a need for the safe attachment and protection that she hoped the social bond with her family might provide. Some runaways turned repeatedly to the family, even after serious physical and emotional ruptures, to attempt reconnection and to get the approval and protection they needed. In Eva's story, the police station became a place of refuge instead of a place to avoid while on the run. Shifts in the nature of the peer bond, community ties, and family connections were all evident in her story.

Jimmy's story was unique because he ran away from foster homes in an attempt to return home to his mother and siblings. He directed his rage at an intrusive social worker who continually broke up his family. His mother "lets me do whatever I want," except "no drugs and no trouble." Jimmy had no problem complying. When asked how he would like things to be, he answered, "I'd be at home for the rest of my life and have a million dollars!" He described his rage at the social worker whom he considered to be a meddler and troublemaker:

> She pulls all kinds of crap. She'll do anything. She lies. . . . We were moving, and we just got there, and things weren't there yet, and things weren't unpacked. She came in and said, "This place is a mess! There's no furniture for the kids; there's no beds!" And she just started. . . . She came back and said the house was wrecked and there was no place for us to sleep. That pissed me off so bad! I swear to God, I don't know what

held me back from hitting her! I was really gonna beat her! She'll do anything to put us away!

The social worker observed a family in what she considered a substandard living situation and placed the children in protective custody. But from the youth's perspective, the community structure interfered in his family's domestic privacy. Jimmy continually ran away from the juvenile facilities to return to what the social service agencies had deemed an inappropriate place for him and his siblings to live. He said, "I hate being in someone else's custody! I hate being told what to do!" The family pull was strong, and Jimmy felt that it was all he needed, beds or no.

This was also the case with another young man who closed ranks with his family against social service providers. Roy lied to the school psychologist about his bruises from beatings by his father, and it wasn't until the neighbors reported the family to the Department of Social Services that he was forcibly removed from his family and placed in protective custody in public juvenile facilities. He continued to run away on a regular basis.[19]

However, not all runaways hold such strong feelings toward their families. Michael was a young person who could not tolerate life in his parents' house. He became animated when he shared how much he liked being at the shelter:

I was locked up, and about four days later, I came here. They don't yell at you here. Usually, [in my family] if you do one thing wrong and then the same thing, they come down pretty hard on you. But here, if you do the same thing wrong, they just go, "Whoa, we're gonna have to work a little bit harder on this." I think they actually bust down on you pretty hard. But here, they'll talk to you. But, if you keep yelling at them, they'll snap back at you! They're like your parents, but they're cool. They're more like your friends. Here they aren't like "staff"—they are like my friends. You'll think, "Oh wow, the night is gonna be great!" With Thomas,[20] we go to the Y, swim, play basketball, lift weights; it's just totally great! With Maria, we go to the movies, and Alfie lets you talk to the girls on Friday and Saturday nights, but if you try anything, you get in trouble! I never try that much.

Michael had a clear vision of what it should be like to be treated fairly and respectfully, and he described it in detail. Michael was able to connect in positive ways with community workers and find the emotional bonding that he sought.

The emotional connections of the social bond in families, among peers, and with the wider community were not predictable or static. Where runaways placed their alliances depended on many subtle influences—emotional, situational, and interactional—based on the alternatives that they perceived. Catalysts for running away cannot be predicted. However, the emotional bonds in the family may form, wither, and reform. Consequently, runaways sought social connections with someone, and their decisions to leave home had these emotional dimensions.

Shifts in Sibling Bonds

The sibling relationship is a unique experience. The role of sibship can be key in a family, whether providing support and a buffer against the conflict with parents, or rivalry and hostility—including incest and physical abuse. The most salient feature in the sibling relationships of runaways was the resilience and flexibility of this emotional social connection. They consistently reported changes in the quality of their interactions with their siblings—from intense passion to disinterested detachment, from rage and hatred to tender protectiveness. The fluid nature of the sibling bond illuminated the restorative nature of family social bonds and the potential possibilities of our social emotional connectedness in general.

One runaway described how her relationship with her brother had changed for her:

> The whole time I was growing up, my brother used to beat on me and all this stuff. . . . When we were younger we just couldn't stand each other. But ever since, 'cause, see, my brother hasn't lived at my house since he was fourteen years old and he just recently moved back in. Now we're just so close—I can trust him, and he'll do anything for me, and I

really . . . and it's good to have him around because when my mom acts up, he can say to my mom, "Listen, you know, you gotta chill out and stop treating her this way!" And then it's not just me, you know, only defending myself . . . (Stacey)

The connection between Stacey and her brother became transformed from one of antagonism and physical altercations to an alliance in which he assisted in the provision of much needed protection for this daughter of an alcoholic, possibly mentally ill mother. Relationships are not immutable. The flexible nature of social connection allowed this young teenager to find in her older brother a necessary ally in the family.

A popular myth (and theory that has driven the sociology of deviance) about runaways is that they are hardened juvenile delinquents. Some, in fact, do arrive at the shelter in shackles and handcuffs, coming directly from locked-down, secured facilities.[21] Yet many of these same runaways expressed tender feelings of protection and concern toward younger siblings left behind at home. They felt guilty for abandoning them, often in physically or sexually abusive situations:

My father gets pissed off, but he doesn't take it out on my little brother anymore. I have seen him kick around my little brother once, and I stood up for my little brother 'cause I didn't want anything to happen to him! (Gregg)

Yeah, my brother's out living with my aunt right now. He just got out of a lockup. My little brother's been in and out of a little mischief. He's been in lockup already; he's not too clean . . . . Actually, I'm feeling kind of like it's my fault, that I'm the one to blame because my oldest brother wasn't around and then all of it was stuck on me for him to look up to, and then he saw how I was doin' it. . . . And then, I just got to feelin' like it was my fault 'cause I knew what I was doing . . . and. . . . Then I got into a nice little talk with him and told him, "Chill— trouble's not gonna get you nowhere." He's like "Well, . . . well." I said, "Trust me, OK? Just trust me." My mom was beatin' my little brother since he was three years old, and I don't understand—throwing him around and stuff. (Jimmy)

For these runaway boys, thoughts of their unprotected younger sibling elicited feelings of tenderness and a desire to keep them from harm. The sibling connection was positive and strong for them and might indicate a capability for further healing and bonding with other family members. Gregg said, "I stood up for my little brother" with pride in his voice. Jimmy's feelings of guilt—"like it was my fault"—prompted him to have a heart-to-heart talk with his baby brother, giving the runaway the opportunity to meet some of the expectations of the older sibling role, such as giving advice, expressing tender concern, or providing protection. That they worried about their family members left behind fleshed out a picture of these youths as more than just "hardened thugs." After all, runaways were often brought in on assault and battery charges and usually were full of resentment and pent-up anger. But the social bond is in motion, and runaways connected to their families in complex emotional ways.

So strong were the feelings of protection for her siblings that one runaway, Jean, went so far as to take her three little brothers and sisters with her:

> I was thirteen years old then. I'm pretty mature for my age, I personally think. Because, like, since I was seven years old, I have been taking care of my little brothers and sisters. I potty-trained my little sister—I did all that stuff. Like, I had the baby since I was seven years old, and I knew what I was doing, you know?
>
> I ran away with my best friend. I was gonna go to a party that night, right? So a friend of mine told me there's a cop at my house saying all this stuff would happen if I went home that night so, well, I'm not going home.
>
> I ended up moving in with my . . . with my boyfriend—he's nineteen years old[22]—down the street. I ended up taking the kids because my parents were getting a divorce and. . . . No problem, I couldn't go to school, but no problem . . .

This youth's sense of loyalty and protectiveness was intact toward her younger siblings, even though this runaway might be seen as a delinquent "bad seed"—she had been picked up by police and charged with status offenses numerous times (runaway and truancy). Jean saw "no problem" with truancy and dropping out of school. She considered honoring the expectations of the older sibling role by caring for her little brothers and sisters as a sign of "maturity" for her young thirteen years. The feelings of tenderness for her younger siblings were a strong pull for Jean, and her commitment to protecting them was stronger than a need to tell the truth, or go to school, or stay in her parent's home. In a parodoxical way, Jean's running away from home, dropping out of school, and lying about her boyfriend's age can be seen as emotionally inspired decision making, whereby she created safety for herself and for those to whom she is loyal in her family.

Parent-Child Connections

In another story of rapprochement, the father made a minor concession in his choice of an outing with his son and bridged a painful gap between them.

Eric ran away from his "controlling and sabotaging" father[23] who always insisted Eric do what his father wanted, which was to play baseball with him. Apparently, his father had been a star pitcher on a local minor league and dreamed of sharing this activity with his son. Eric's father had a master's degree; Eric said his mother worked "five jobs" and is a "very stressed-out woman." Eric described a typical exhausting day of his mother's, which included her "waking everybody up at seven o'clock," working until late at night, and sleeping in her spare time and on her "one day off a week." Eric used drugs—pot and LSD—and spent a summer in a drug rehabilitation program. This middle-class family's approach to child rearing and expectations for their son weighed heavily on Eric. His parent's marriage was intact, and he had two younger sisters; he was the oldest child in this family from a rural part of a New England state. He claimed to have run away "several" times, and at the time of the interview, he had been on a two-week run. No physical or sexual abuse was reported in his family. Eric, a slight, acne-faced seventeen-year-old, carefully depicted the fluid nature of his emotional connection with his father:

> Well, it used to be really good with my dad; we got along well. Things just changed. Really, my dad wanted me to be some-

thing I wasn't, something . . . he was this big baseball champion—he's a second best in the United States! He wanted to see me, you know—I told him I wasn't ready for it. I told him I didn't want to do it! I started doing drugs and stuff, and when you start doing drugs—it just altered how I felt about him.

Well, he didn't really bring me to the baseball field very much. It was usually my choice, but I did it to make him more happy. I did it because I liked to spend time with him, and, you know, he didn't ever like to do anything. . . . I'm an excellent pool player; I'm thinking about going professional! My dad hates pool. I like soccer; my dad hates soccer. He would never play with me, so I figured I would find something if I didn't already have it, stick with it so I could spend time with my dad. He hated to go fishing; he said he used to go all the time. He doesn't mind it now, but he didn't really like it when I was growing up.

Sunday was the first time I've seen him. . . . I talked to him and it was pretty good. We went out. We went fishing and talked about all this stuff. It was pretty good. I had a good time, you know. He won't let me back home but that's . . . because he doesn't feel I'll get along there. He's afraid of something that I'll do. He's afraid I'll hurt my mom or sisters or something. I'm not a violent person at all. I don't know. I really don't know what he thinks, but whatever he thinks, he thinks pretty strongly. He's strongly against my coming back home.

It's a little painful, but I just blame myself on that. That's my fault, not his. Yeah, he understands, but at the same time—it's intense because, he's like, "What the hell, you're my son—you're supposed to stick by me!" and I wasn't. I was off doing my own thing—drugs, basically.

Eric's father insisted on doing what he wanted with his son and that his son was "supposed to stick by" him. As Eric talked about how his father "hates soccer" and "hates pool," I noted sadness and a hurt tone in his voice. As soon as the father leaned in Eric's direction by sharing an activity that Eric enjoyed—fishing—his son warmed up to feeling the loving father-son connection.

But Sunday we went fishing; that was two days ago! That was really fun. We just shot the shit, you know . . .

Eric's father encouraged Eric to participate in the activities that the father believed his son should undertake, such as baseball. After the fishing outing—a nod in the direction of his son's interests—Eric expressed happiness and joy at being able to "shoot the shit" with his strict dad. Eric's running away from home represented a rupture of the family bond, but occasionally, the possibility arises to mend the family connection. This is due, in part, to the malleable nature of emotional bonds.

When seventeen-year-old Megan's mother changed her behavior, life improved for the teenager. Due to her divorced parents' erratic addictive behavior, Megan had been moved in and out of her alcoholic father's and mother's houses and foster families since she was eleven years old. Her parents were both white working-class people who lived in a rural region; her mother was "graduating from college this year"; her father graduated from high school and worked at a public utilities company. Megan's story showed that if parents improve their lives, it can enhance the emotional connection with their children:

I remember that my mom used to party now and then. She'd come home at two o'clock in the morning with her friends. I was in fifth grade, and I used to stay up until two in the morning just to see who she came home with—if she came home with a guy—and then I'd go to bed just to make sure she's OK, you know. But I was only in fifth grade, so I wasn't going to really say anything. And then when we went to Westmont she kind of thought I would straighten out, but she had a steady boyfriend who beat me up. . . . [laugh] Then she was with that other guy—so that was better and she didn't go out as much. And then she finally met this guy, and then they started going out. They were together a long time, and she's gotten a lot a lot better since I moved out. She got her GED and she's going to college, and she's going to graduate this year, and she's a lot better mom than she was when I was little. She doesn't go out at all; she doesn't drink at all—I don't know if she still does pot at all . . .

The runaway experience might lead people to believe that the American family is dissolving beyond repair. However, by studying the dynamic activity of our emotional connections, one can deduce that as long as there are tears and words, there is, in some families, an opportunity for runaways to reattach lovingly to family members. The hopefulness of the runaways' accounts of healing and rapprochement provides social science with material to disprove a cynical argument that youths and families are "beyond reach." We need to know more about family dynamics—emotional and social—to better understand the methods that, as emotional bonds form and dissolve, runaway youths use to decide where to place their allegiance and trust. We are learning that these are emotional decisions and that the runaways resolve their moral crises of trust as best they can, given the alternatives society provides.

CONCLUSION

When I asked runaways to tell me how they ended up in a shelter, they described their confusion as they tried to make sense of emotional struggles in their families. They gave varied reasons for running away from home, falling loosely into four groups: physical, sexual, and/or ritual abuse; overly strict parents; general emotional family conflict; and circumstances in which the youth was pushed out or abandoned and later fled various social service placements.[24] Although the reasons that they cited vary, as did their reactions to particular circumstances, one consistent theme in the interviews was the depth of feeling and the need to be connected and protected, preferably in the family of origin.

Paradoxically, running away from home may be seen as a desperate search for emotional connection. I used Hirschi's (1985) notion of the social bond to describe the emotional social connection that the runaways articulated. Their accounts show that this connection is dynamic and in motion: it can form or weaken, rupture, become damaged beyond repair, or strengthen and heal. Runaway behavior was a manifestation of the rupture of the social bond in the family.

Runaways reported family conflict that reflects a weakening of the bond; their running away, in turn, reflects a rupture of the bond. Often, in cases of physical and sexual abuse, the family rupture was beyond repair. However, there were also stories of strengthening and healing in the family that indicated the possibility for positive outcomes for some runaways and their families.

Utilizing the interactionist perspective provided insight about, and a focus on the meaning of, the interactions in runaways' stories. Applying ideas from sociology of emotion, such as giving importance to emotions as behavioral motivators, revealed that feelings—such as sadness and rejection, for example—played a key role in runaways' constructions of self and in the way they judged the compulsion to struggle to meet norms and expectations in the family.[25] In this way, I found that studying the emotional interactions illuminated the fluidity and dynamism of the bond that influenced the decision to run away.

Runaways saw flight from their families as the best and only option. Given the alternatives they perceived that they had, this choice was part of a process of social weakening of the family bond, and it happened when their expectations for acceptance and protection in the family were continually disappointed. The runaway decision had an emotional dimension, and the choices that the runaways related in the interviews were emotionally motivated. Their decision to run was influenced by the rage, hurt, fear, and disappointment they felt as they struggled in their family relationships. Regardless of the reasons, feelings were heartfelt and overwhelming. They continually shared what they believed to be unsolvable problems with their parents, that is, solvable only by absenting themselves from the home. The interviews revealed a combination of cognitive reasoning and emotional expression that made up their moral struggles to figure out ways to best meet their needs for attachment and connection. Being on the run was a process of seeking places that provided protection and met the needs of attachment and social bonding that the runaways decided could not be met inside family structures.

This chapter contained discussions of the emotional interactions within the family that explained the runaway experience using a microinteractional approach. In Chapter 4, I widen the focus to an examination of the forces that influence feeling life, with a conflict view of the position of the runaways in social structures. I will show that interactions from the subordinate position that runaways perceive themselves to occupy—a powerlessness under authority in the family, at school, with the police, and in the social service system—produce resentment and anger aimed uncharacteristically "upward" toward that authority. Analyzing this "one-down" power position—and the resultant emotions that it produces—reveal further complex influences in the decision to runaway.

Hitchhiker

Can I get a ride to the bus depot?
Can I get a ride to the bus?

I got to get myself out of this town.
I say I got to get out of town.

I ain't got much money saved up, you see.
I ain't got much money to save.

Yeah sure I want myself a job.
Yeah sure I'll do any job.

What's that you say you want me to play?
What's that you want me to play?

You say for every button you'll give me a buck;
so every button's worth a buck.

You say you need to hear I'm eighteen,
that for a ride, tell you eighteen.

No problem, sir, because I am eighteen,
eighteen years old and no longer green.

I'll play your game to get a ride.
I'll do as you say—see, I don't mind.

I'll unsnap, unhinge, and unzip—
so long as you help me on my trip.

Just one thing sir, before I play:
isn't the bus depot the other way?

David Keiser

97

Chapter 4

The Politics of Anger: Rebellion, *Ressentiment,* and Emotional Capital

You know, my dad tried to make everything really structured for me, and I hated it! I couldn't stand it! I was like, "Dad, get away from me! I don't need this!" He made me want to do more drugs 'cause he was structuring my time, and I was like, every second I got, I would get drugs! I went out and got drugs 'cause my time was so structured that I never thought I'd be able to do anything anymore! Before you know it, I was going through half an ounce a week! That's a lot of pot you know, and Jesus! My dad caught on, you know . . .

Most of the kids I grew up with used drugs—ever since I was six years old, you know. When I was thirteen years old, I just stole a joint from my dad. I was never really popular—I never really had any friends. I went to this prep school, but I was a stoner . . .

I was pretty pissed at my foster parents—I took off; I left; I went out and got stoned and came back afterwards. I told them I was pissed off so bad I had to get away, you know? I couldn't stay there, but they let me stay there until I found another foster home. They had been really nice to me, you know? It's just that I messed up so bad, they couldn't forgive me for it. I lied to them; I broke every rule in the book. I said, all right—I understand. We had a long talk. I was pretty close to my foster parents, but not close enough I guess. I probably lied a lot. [Awaiting placement with another foster family.]

Eric, age seventeen

INTRODUCTION

Youth behavior is heavily regulated—legally and socially. In every structure in which they relate, young people occupy a subordinate position—in families, at schools, in the eyes of the police and organizations in the wider community. Except among peers and with siblings, young people are dominated by some authority. Youths often perceive the use of that authority as unjust, unfair, and arbitrary. These perceptions of injustice, coupled with the struggle to meet the norms and expectations of those controlling and regulating structures, produces strain and tension between youths and authority figures. It also produces an internal struggle in which youths must decide whether to attempt to meet the expectations of what they consider to be unfair conditions. Running away is behavior that seeks to alleviate this tension and resolve the struggle. Anger stemming from this powerlessness within society was apparent in the interviews with runaways.

Teenage runaways display considerable anger and defiance. What role do such emotions play in runaway behavior? In this chapter, I will focus on running away as a rebellious response to powerlessness, motivated by feelings of anger, resentment, and disappointment. In the first section, I will present the emotional responses that result when youths perceive that adults wield unfair, unjust, and arbitrary authority over them. Next, I will present examples of the emotional and moral dilemma that runaways face concerning whether to disobey their abusive parents or adhere to the norms in families that they believed did not meet their needs. Then I present a framework demonstrating that a simmering *ressentiment* and their analysis of their victimology form an "emotional capital" that youths draw on to empower them to "throw off the yoke of conformity," which they felt was choking them in their families—and then run away. In the last two sections, a philosophy of anger and insubordination and ideas about the politics of the aim of anger frame a presentation of the runaways' defiant and disobedient angry behavior. Throughout this chapter, the runaways defend their behavior as fight-back action against disadvantage and disempowerment. I will argue that, in some ways, their "bad attitude" is all these teenagers really have in situations with people whom they perceive to devalue and discount their youthful expressions and needs.

A UNANIMOUS CHORUS BY THE RULED:
"TOO MANY UNFAIR RULES AND RULERS"

Laws and regulations limit many transactions in which youths are allowed to participate. For example, minors may not rent a dwelling, sign a legal document such as a lease, purchase property, or open a bank account on their own before the age of eighteen. Statutes that affect young people vary by federal, state, and local mandate, but a partial list of behaviors subject to age restriction (which, therefore, can become status offenses) includes the following:

Age (years)	Legal Activity
13	Eligibility to be tried as a felon
15½	Obtain a driving permit
16	Operate a motor vehicle
16	Work for pay in a public establishment
16	Marry
17	Public curfew
18	Vote
18	Serve in the armed forces
18	Purchase cigarettes
21	Purchase alcohol
21	Sign contracts; inherit

As contemporary adolescents move through the stage between childhood and the attainment of adult status, laws that govern their behavior are in place for their protection. There is historical precedence for protective legislation on behalf of American youths. "Kiddie" pornographers prey upon street youths today, much in the same way that industrialists a century ago rounded up children to employ in dank factories and mercilessly overwork them. Historians trace the emergence, development, and changes in public legislation that have affected children (Aries, 1962; Kett, 1997; Modell and Goodman, 1990; Levine and White, 1994; Glick, 1994). Differing reasons for youths' protection have evolved over time, paralleling changes in the meaning of "adolescence" (Modell and Goodman, 1990, p. 93). For

example, the introduction of child labor laws was a protective mea-
sure for children during the industrialization period in the United
States. However, today, in a period of economic distress, many of the
regulations regarding young people's access to work are perceived
by them to be outdated. In 1990, 17.3 percent of adolescents, ages
twelve to seventeen, of all races lived in poverty (U.S. Bureau of the
Census, 1992, p. 48).[1] Young people are not allowed to work before
the age of sixteen (depending on local statutes), so they hit the streets
in search of "odd jobs," and they find them. Unfortunately, some
youths find their way into drug dealing, illicit sexual activity, and
other crimes. Denied access to legitimate means of earning money,
some of these youths living in poverty may turn to illegitimate
means. Although I'm not advocating a return to child labor, young
people's access to economic structures could be reexamined in light
of the contemporary economic environment.

Youth cultures influences youth behavior. Many young people
seem sophisticated and sexually precocious, and they believe their
preference for more autonomy is being discounted. These youths
mimic adult behavior early in their lives. On television, adults from
the commercial sphere feed the youth market nudity, sexual sophis-
tication, and sexualized music videos, even as teenagers report feeling constrained by early curfews and old-fashioned sexual norms
(Rubin, 1994; p. 157). Psychologist and educator Francis Ianni
notes that we live in an "age-graded caste" system (1989, p. 7).
Statutes such as age of eligibility for working, curfews, and even
purchasing cigarettes, it can be argued, are becoming anachronistic
and outmoded. What was once instituted as protective has come to
be seen as overly restrictive. Runaways' desire for more autonomy
and their complaints about a lack of control over many areas in their
own lives are recurring themes in their stories.

The majority of the young people who participated in this study
protested what they perceived as overly protective parents, abusive
adults, and general unfairness in family and foster family household
rules. Many of these youths seemed quite mature and already sexually active. Even at thirteen years old, they claimed to know exactly
what they wanted to wear, where they needed to go, what they
wanted to do—in general, they considered themselves capable of
organizing their lives. Yet runaways reported that they felt they had

virtually no voice in decisions made in their conflicted families concerning the governing of their behavior, and they resented parents and adults meddling in what they considered to be their personal affairs.

For runaways, the relationship to authority was central. In almost every social structure that they occupy, they were subordinate. Within the family (except for younger siblings), their parents, uncles and aunts, grandparents, and older siblings wield decision-making power over them. At school, the principal, teachers, and all other school personnel may reprimand them at any time. In the community, the police, social workers, storekeepers—all had authority over young people's movements and activities. This is how study participants felt about social workers, police, and parents deciding their fate:

> My mom doesn't even really have any say over me—my social worker pretty much decides what he thinks is gonna be best for me—but he doesn't even talk to me! He doesn't know what I'm like, and I tell him what I am looking for, in a place to stay. . . . Well, what I wanted was a nice foster home to stay at, 'cause I really don't like the program setting, you know, with things like so many people here, and you really can't go out and do anything—you have no freedom at all! And he—he wants to send me to, you know, a place that's all girls and you—the place he's thinking about is an alternative to lockup? I really . . . [nervous laugh] I don't need to go there, you know? And you have to ask to stand up and stuff, and it's like [nervous laugh], Great! [sarcastic] (Eva)

> 'Cause with all the places I've been, I'd rather not take the chances of getting sent back to them. I hate being sent away! I hate being in someone else's custody! I hate being told what to do, 'cause I'm not used to being told what to do. My mom *asks* me to do things; she doesn't tell me! She *asks* me to take out the trash; she *asks* me to clean up my room; she *asks* me if sometimes I could help her with somethin'. She asks me *not* to do things, too—like she asks me not to swear . . . (Jimmy)

LaWanda, a twelve-year-old African-American–Puerto Rican runaway, told about her experiences with the police and her physical altercations with her social worker. LaWanda violated her probation with a stolen car charge—"I didn't know it was stolen." I was unable to ascertain what the original offense was that earned her probation. LaWanda's mother was a twenty-five-year-old African American with a ninth-grade education. LaWanda had a younger sister who would be ten years old, which made LaWanda's mother a mother of two children at age fifteen. Her father was in jail, "he just went in"—LaWanda saw him recently. LaWanda lived in a nearby city with her sixty-three-year-old grandmother (her mother's mother) whenever the court and her social workers would allow it. Last time she was in court, the judge recommended a Department of Youth Service placement in lockup for her—she reported that she ran away from there.

LaWanda related that her relationship with her mother was problematic. LaWanda said that her mother and she had conflicts, but the circumstances were not clear:

> We fight. She's always hit me, but I was scared to say something to her. It don't feel like nothin' to me now. I don't know, we just can't get along. We can't talk. Like we see each other, but we don't make any special trips to see each other. She goes to my grandmother's house with my aunt—she'll stay in the car, and I wave at her, but I ain't gonna stop and talk to her. 'Cause I ain't got nuttin' to say to her. 'Cause every time I got somethin to say, it goin' be bad anyway. I just keep goin' my way. She don't say nothin'.

LaWanda wore an eerie smirk as she related her account of being in police custody:

> Like the cops, yesterday they were telling me to shut up, and I'm like, "Hold up!" They cops, they can put me where they want, tellin' me, "Hold up and sit there and be quiet!" I had got up to look at something, 'cause you know how they got the wanted ads up on the wall? And he's all, "Sit down, now!" And I looked at him, and I'm talking about, oh God . . . last time—what was that—oh, I had asked 'em if they could turn on the light, 'cause I like to see the light [on top of the police car] and they say, "No, shut up!" And I said, "Whyn't you

make me shut up!" I said it just like that! Not even my parents tell me to shut up! Cop or no cop. . . . They tryin' to threaten me with that, "You wanna stay here behind these bars?" They can't do to that to me! So I said, "Yup!" They can't do that to you, all right? I already know that they can't do that to you— put me behind bars because they were telling me to shut up? Then they handcuffing me. That's all I got to say. I really don't care. They can't do that much to me—what they gonna do, keep me in there for life? That's why I try not to argue with the staff here.

LaWanda sat in front of me, her arms folded across her chest and her jaw jutting out in a tight, angry manner. Underlying LaWanda's belief system was a commitment to the social hierarchy of police above citizen and to the rules of a fair legal system. It wasn't that she believed in lawlessness or no authority. LaWanda recognized and honored notions of justice and legality. "They can't do that!" she said, referring to the police keeping her in jail "for life." She had a concise vision of what was fair, just, and, in her mind, legal. LaWanda knew it would be "illegal" for the police to keep her in jail, especially for something as inconsequential as responding with indignation to them telling her to "Shut up!" LaWanda's sense of her self-dignity and self-worth were intact as she said, "Cop or no cop"—nobody gets away with talking to LaWanda like that! Not even her parents speak to her with such disrespect, she reported, although it isn't clear from her story what "parents" she was referring to. Her defiant lack of deference to what she perceived as a harsh authority can be seen as an expression of her own sense of self-worth:

That's why I try not to argue with anybody 'cause it can get serious. If they ever touch me, I'll hit them back! If I don't like you, and I tell you, "Don't touch me!" and you touch me—I'm gonna hit you! Like my social worker, I told her not to touch me because she lied to me so much! When I first even got put in lockup, she would tell me I am going back to my gramma's house! She told my grandmother I was coming back too! So they didn't let me call my grandmother, and she didn't know where I was. And my social worker, 'fore I came here, we got into a big argument! I was trying to get out of the car, to talk to my probation officer, and she tried to push my head getting in the car—and I hit her! I told her not to touch me! 'Cause they got the right to restrain you, but hey—it's me and some three other social workers come up on me . . .

LaWanda seemed to be fighting a losing battle to gain respect and understanding from the community agents with whom she came into contact. Her style of rebelliousness and the physically assaultive manner that she utilized assured her of being in situations in which adults would not honor her with the care and tenderness she sought. Her simmering rage and "threatening demeanor" evoked the very behavior from authority figures that confirmed her powerlessness. Police and social service workers responded to LaWanda's defiance with even more authoritarian and regulative behavior. These interactions produced a rage in LaWanda and a sense of indignation at unjust treatment. She reported feeling furious about the arbitrary manner in which she perceived authority was wielded over her; she was angry, too, at what she felt were the injustices in the confrontations in her life. LaWanda was a bright, emotionally and morally intact young person who was caught up in a power drama, some of which was not her making. The police, social workers, and adult family members with whom she came into contact played right into her defiant drama, continually proving her point that authority figures and community agents can be inflexible, stern, and severe.

Except when among peers and younger siblings, runaways often felt forced to deal with the difficulty of handling relationships and situations in which they believed they had no voice. Overwhelmingly, they reported instances of what they perceived to be unjust and rigid wielding of authority over them. Here are a few of their comments:

I don't want to go to my house because my curfew will be at 7:00 p.m., and it will be hard for me. Because I will be in school until 5:00 p.m. and then—that's "Party Time!," hanging out with friends . . . (Carmen)

I think that I should be able to have a say in who my friends are. I don't think that my mom should have the right to tell me who is my friend because I'm at the age to know who I should hang out with and who I shouldn't! If I make a bad choice, then I have to deal with that—she doesn't. Yeah, she knows how I feel, but she thinks I'm going to come home pregnant, and I'm gonna get AIDS! She's scared that I'm going to make a lot of bad choices, but I don't think I will. (Amy)

I got tired of my mom telling me, "You can't do this, and you can't do that!" and "I don't want you to be with him!" My mom was fifteen years old and she was going out with someone who was twenty years old, but she sees so much wrong with me going out with my boyfriend who's only three years older than me! (June)

My dad has punished me in the fucking queerest ways! He's put me in a chair and made me sit there for the whole day! Or made me go in my room. I was in my room twenty-four hours a day on the weekends—I never came out! I'd go upstairs and punch holes in my wall; I'd be so pissed off about him yelling at me for no reason! I never did anything wrong—I always did my schoolwork! He reacted like I didn't do my schoolwork, 'cause I was getting As and Bs, and as soon as I came here, they went down, but I'm bringing them back up a lot now. I've been getting projects in, doing my work. But, say you didn't do your schoolwork, a normal punishment for that would be to ground you for a day or something, go to your room for a half hour. They make me go to my room for a week! I was grounded. I didn't come out of my room—I wasn't able to watch TV for a whole school year! (Gregg)

But see—while I was running away, my friends' parents would get kinda sick of feeding me, and I couldn't go to school because my Social Security number and my name and all these other things. And I couldn't get a job because of my Social Security number—because they ask for your Social Security number and date of birth and all that other stuff! So, I don't want to be living off somebody, not even being able to go to school, or pay them or anything. . . . (Anne)

A range of emotions was produced in response to interactions regarding runaways' sense of too many unfair rules in their lives. One youngster exclaimed, "It will be hard for me" because she will miss "Party Time!" Even though this may seem frivolous to adults, when youths socialize among their peers, they grow, change, and experience themselves. Young people develop their sense of self and identity inside peer groups (Dusek, 1991, p. 305). The application of what they felt were arbitrary curfews, "getting grounded," and not being allowed to go out or have friends come over produced extremely angry feelings—enough sometimes to be cited as reasons for running away from home. For many youths, the guidance and parenting offered by parents and adults was perceived as over-restrictive. It seemed that the runaways wanted less restriction in their ability to choose their own friends and their own romantic partners—another situation that angered runaways. "I'm at the age to know" was an expression full of resentment and irritation. "I got tired of my mom telling me" (which boyfriend to go out with) was a statement reflecting the frustration that another young girl felt with what she believed was her mother's hypocritical parenting (because her mother had gone out with an older fellow).[2]

For the disgruntled runaways in this sample, negotiating together with parents and guardians—setting house rules, deciding which friendships are acceptable, and picking what time curfews ought to be—rarely came up as an experience they shared. One boy "punches holes in walls" for being sent to his room "for no reason." Gregg said he's "pissed off," but upon closer regard, he seemed to be feeling sad and rejected—"staying in the room all weekend." Furthermore, he carefully explained what he perceived would be fair treatment and what wouldn't. Anne reported feeling frustrated and hopeless at trying to sort out the mechanics of surviving on the run—her Social Security number, getting a job, maneuvering through school—her voice trailed off in irritation.

Throughout the study, runaways repeatedly offered to "face the consequences" of their misbehavior, giving examples and ideas for what they felt constituted fair punishment. Many youths in the sample displayed a sense of moral justice and commitment to normative conforming behavior. They were responding with fury to what they considered to be unfair and unjust treatment, not to simply being punished. They did not report that they wanted to roam free with no rules; they instead related that they wanted to have a say in developing what they considered to be fair rules.

One clever, fourteen-year-old, African-American urban youth, Evander, said that he ran away because he wanted to have a good time. "Life is for having fun—I don't want to grow old, all crusty!" he confided with an impish grin:

> I left because I was hanging out with my friends. I didn't want to come in the house that early—I come in the house when I get tired! I'll mind my mom when I'm ready. That's how I feel. I'll do all the rules, but when I'm ready! It's not that I didn't want to mind. I just didn't want to come in. She'd be like, "Come in the house at five o'clock." Five o'clock! and stay for good? The day's still early! When I'm out, having fun, making money, hanging out, talking to girls—it's fun, it's a lot—a lot goes on.

Evander was resentful at what he considered overly strict parenting. However, he revealed that he "deals rock" (sells crack cocaine) and doesn't come home for days on end. Evander was from nearby New Haven—he lived either at his mother's house or with his father and stepmother. He had seven siblings between the two families. He came into the shelter from serving a one-month sentence in a secured facility—his mother put a "stubborn CHINS" on him. He had run away from home and hadn't called or alerted his mother of his whereabouts. "She didn't really care—she was just worried," was how he described his mother's attitude toward his running away, even though she had called the police to report him missing. Thirty years old, Evander's mother worked in the office of a large national company; his father was a thirty-one-year-old high school graduate and unemployed.

Evander didn't discuss his feelings about the divorce between his parents, the situations in the two different households, or his relationships with his siblings. Resentment surfaced when he spoke of "minding his mother." Evander would do it—but at his own pace.

Evander's tone changed as he spoke of having to obey. I could hear the defiance in his rising voice. He said he's "not really angry" at his mother:

> In a way, yeah, cause, she won't let me get bailed out. My father would let me get out. I would like to go to my father's house. It's better—I just like my father better; he understands me better. My ma told the court, "No, Don't let him go" to my dad. I wouldn't have been in lockup more than half an hour . . .

Beneath the veneer of just "having fun," for Evander, there simmered resentment at his mother's rules and possibly fear and hurt feelings.

Rage at perceived injustice was central for one participant, fifteen-year-old Isaiah. Isaiah expressed an almost palpable anguish and intensity of passion as he talked about his life. His sense of the injustice and futility of his situation was ever-present in his comments and in the topics he chose to divulge. This boy told of his many travails in his foster home placement:

> Well, I'll get angry, but it's deep inside. I never show it on the outside. I never yell and get all crazy, and I never show it to you. But I could tell you how angry I get—real angry! I get so mad sometimes, I just start sweatin'. I just sit down and think about things and just start flinchin'. Flinchin', flinchin'—oh my God—just thinking about, wow, what could happen, what could happen . . .
>
> I called my social worker and I begged him to [move me from this foster home]. I didn't like it, so I left, because the lady treated me like I was some kind of robot. They had five little kids in that house and she was just using me as her slave. "Grab that! Do the laundry! Out of my way!" I'll do anything, but she went overboard! Keep me in the house all day! Five other foster kids and they were all boys—healthy boys—and I can't understand that I just had to do it all.
>
> I mean, I'm just—what really ticked me off was when she told me to take the dishes out of the dishwasher and put them in the sink, wash them again, and then put them back in the dishwasher! I thought she was stupid! "No, I'm not doing it!"

And she said, "Well, if you're not doing it, then you're going to leave!" And I'm packing my bag and she wouldn't let me take my clothes along! "You're not taking your clothes until I get paid!" And I thought she was doing it for me, but you know all these foster kids that are coming in there—so I left. I didn't care, I went to a friend's house and stayed the night. I called my social worker in the morning, and we went to court . . .

There was no doubt in Isaiah's mind that, for him, this dishwashing incident was an unfair, arbitrary wielding of authority. The resentment he felt about this motivated his decision to leave and to call his social worker for assistance. This teenager was making the "right" judgment, against the "right" people, according to one of Western civilization's great thinkers, Aristotle. He wrote, in the *Nicomachean Ethics*, the following apt phrase:

> [anyone] who does not get angry when there is reason to be angry, or does not get angry in the right way at the right time and with the right people, is a dolt. (cited in Spelman, 1989, p. 263)

Looking at the lives of many teenagers using Aristotle's lens begs the question, "Why aren't more youths furious and running away?" Considering that almost all youths are under some kind of authority, why don't they all feel rebellious? Because life in most families is not like life in the families of these runaways. For the majority of families, authority is combined with love and respect, which allows young people to feel safe and protected and affords them an opportunity to learn how to become responsible adults (Janus et al., 1987, p. 21). Unfortunately, for the young people who are forced by the system to pass through the shelter, this is not the case. However, even the shelter is an improvement over the ultimate nightmare for many runaways arriving from the Department of Youth Services with status offenses: lockup.

THE ULTIMATE WIELDING OF AUTHORITY OVER YOUTHS: "LOCKUP IS HELL"

Lockup was described by the runaways in one word: "hell." Violent or serious criminal youth offenders are transported to locked-down juvenile facilities. Some youths are sentenced to be held there until they turn eighteen years old; others are released after short-term sentences. Only two youths in this study chose to speak about lock-up, and then only briefly:

> It was like hell! Lockup was boring. How do you explain it? . . . you can't see outside, you can't breathe fresh air. You're locked up! You do what they tell you to do. Some of them are so mean—some of them beat us up bad! They spit in your food! They feed you horse and stuff—nasty raccoon meat and stuff! (Evander)

> I was supposed to be there for a year, but they let me out on a suspended [sentence]. I was only supposed to go to court to get my bail money, and they locked me up! I don't know why! Every time I go to court, they don't give me a chance—they just lock me up! They give me a suspended license, if I don't cooperate. They wanted me to get a trial. They wanted me to do nothing else, so then you got to fight for that trial—and I'm not going to plead guilty! They locked me up! I told my caseworker. I came out innocent. If I wouldn't have pleaded for a trial, I would have been guilty and I would have stayed in the lockup—which is hell! It looks like a jail, and they got bars on the windows. You can't go out; you can't call nobody; you can't do nothing; you have to clean—all they have is clean! You have to eat or you get grounded, you get penalties, what-ever you call that; in some of them—in Hartford—you have to ask permission to stand up! We went to school there—we had to. (Isabel)

Isabel was an angry Latina who ran away from an extremely abusive father. She preferred to speak Spanish and misunderstood English. Her story was full of anguish and resentment at what she perceived to be unjust treatment she had received at the hands of those in authority over her—her physically abusive father, her so-cial worker (who doesn't seem to protect her in juvenile court), the bureaucracy of the lockup system. According to Aristotle, she was appropriately angry at the appropriate people.

Runaways reported that they believed there were too many rules, and too many of them were unfair. Their narratives showed that they responded to the interactions regarding the regulation of their lives with anger and defiance. Perceiving themselves as without a voice, they did not believe they could effect satisfactory changes in their family situations. They felt that they had to simply withstand maltreatment and injustice until they were eighteen years old, or until they could not stand it anymore. The next section explores their confusion and their dilemma: how to live under what they perceive as inequitable conditions.

STRUGGLES TO MEET EXPECTATIONS: "I LOVE MY MOTHER, BUT . . . "

Thus far, we have seen that for young people, many aspects of their lives are closely regulated legally and socially. Adolescents are in the subordinate position in many, if not all, social structures in which they interact. Youths in this study expressed outrage and indignation at what they perceived as unfair and arbitrary setting and enforcement of rules. This anger and resentment simmers and builds as the youths perceive the injustices done to them and realize their powerlessness over their ability to ameliorate their status.

Add to this confusion another emotional dilemma: the moral struggle of the adolescents trying to meet the norms and expectations of the controlling and regulating institutions. As much as these youths felt angry and hurt at the injustices done to them by parents and police, they also yearned to be involved in structures that did meet their needs. Thus, they reported a confusion over whether to disobey their parents or adhere to family norms. Many of the runaways painted emotional pictures of their confusion as arising from expectations they had for how a mother "should act," or how a family "should be." "How it is versus how it should be" was a theme in many of the life accounts of runaways, expressed in emotions such as disappointment and resentment. The youths revealed their struggles and emotion work, saying, "I love my mother, but . . . ":

I had totally no respect for her 'cause. . . . I'd never hit her, there's that respect, but—I love her, but—I didn't like her. I don't trust her anymore; my respect for her is down to a .3, you know? (Princess)

I don't know. I'm confused about it. Really confused. If I have a problem, I can go to her and she listens and stuff, but if there's something I want—she already has her mind made up about it! If she says, "No, you can't go here, you can't go there," then I'm just like, "Look, sit down and be quiet and let me say everything I have to say about it." But she already has her mind made up, and the answer's always the same—"No!" I could never say that I hate my mom, 'cause I do love her, but it's wicked hard for me to deal with right now. (June)

I want to know—if I were to leave, where is the best place I can go? I don't want to be at my mom's 'cause we get in physical fights, and I don't want to deal with that. I miss her, but—she can only look at her point of view; she never looks at mine so . . . I don't want to be with my mom. I don't want to put up with everything that she does. I don't want to be with her because she's makes my life hell. She just hurts everything that I have. (Megan)

These young people were sorting out their confused feelings of love and anger, need and hurt—trying to comprehend the paradox of opposing emotions they held toward their parents. This emotional confusion sometimes led to their running away. Expectations between parents and children were often romanticized by both parties, but the struggle, confusion, and disappointment were real. As difficult family interactions occurred, young people were weighing their options and experiencing their feelings, trying to sort out the best alternative to solving what was, in their view, irresolvable conflict. Being treated unfairly, but not really having the "right" to hate their oppressor, placed the youths in untenable situations. The normative expectation in the family, "Thou Shalt Love Thy Father and Mother," presented a moral and emotional challenge to children of parents who were, for example, sexually and physically assaulting them.

Running away can be seen as the culmination of this emotional struggle—a decision influenced by hurt feelings, resentment, confusion, and disappointment. Escalating confusion and mistrust toward the parent, coupled with a sense of perceived injustice, and finally ignited by a severe argument or violent incident between the adolescent and the parent was a typical pattern evidenced in these stories. Running away was seen an act of rebellion—an outburst that reflected the maltreated adolescents' built up emotions of resentment and disappointment.

However, running away behavior did not always stem from an emotional crisis. Another way the behavior evolved was as the culmination of a slow, prolonged struggle. One fifteen-year-old Latino runaway, soon to be a father, expressed this struggle in a confused sorting out of competing norms. He lived at home with his mother, who did not go to school and did not know how to write, according to Carlos. His father was in jail. His eighteen-year-old girlfriend was pregnant. Although Carlos talked about drug dealing and stealing car radios, he thought that "everybody" (society) should:

> pay the mind to more jobs and more malls. And give us jobs, even if we do got a record, give us a job! At least trust us! There will be less violence and less drugs on the street then. The problem is that all my friends on the street is violent.

Carlos was awaiting a trial on criminal charges for a stolen vehicle:

> You grow up fast, especially when you're out on the streets. You gotta grow up: if you don't, you die, or something happens to you. I don't know, it's like, I had a best friend die, and I just promised to myself that before they take my life, I'm gonna take theirs. I always told myself that. All my friends are part of my family—I grew up with them and I'll stick to them the rest of my life. I understand that now I got two people to worry about, but if I don't die by the time I'm twenty years old, it's for my kid—I wanna be there for my kid.
>
> See, my dad wasn't there for me, so by the time he [my kid] my age, he can understand. "Oh daddy didn't do that. I ain't gonna do that either!" I'm gonna show my kid, "Do this!" Like, um, I told my dad, "Dad, how come you never talk to me?" And he goes, like, "I just want you to learn it yourself." By the time I was eleven years old, I started smoking the weed, break-

ing in houses, taking radios from cars! By the time I hit thirteen years old, I started dealing drugs. It went good for awhile. . . . But, I don't I think when he comes out [of prison]—he wanted me to learn all this on my own, the hard way . . .

Carlos struggled with meeting the expectations of being a son, a father, a gang member, and a member of a larger society. An underlying tension existed in his story. Something was amiss as he talked about how much he loved to be in the streets of New Haven with his gang buddies and ended up running away and in trouble with the law. On the one hand, he reported loving his mother, girlfriend, and baby-on-the-way very deeply, and when he spoke of them, his voice lowered dramatically and was filled with emotion. But then he would sit up and talk about his street peers, detailing how he stole car radios and sold drugs. He would become really emotional and animated when he discussed these two things: his passion for his friends and his mother and girlfriend—the latter almost always in the same breath! He exhibited deep passion when he talked about his mother and the mother of his child, but he continually ended up out on the street with his buddies. His confusion over conflicting feelings as he attempted to meet the expectations of being a good son, a good father, and a true friend mounted and led him to, as he expressed it—"p-h-h-ht! I'm outta there!"—make another emotionally charged run from his mother's house.

Scheff describes the advantage of using "contextual meaning" to decipher emotion language—when the actor uses a word "invented on the spur of the moment to fulfill the expression that is needed" (1990, p. 39). "Ph-h-h-h-t!" was Carlos' sound expression of "I gotta go—the pressure is on me." The emotional strain on this young man must have been intense at this period of his life. Not quite an adult himself, and not having an adult male to guide and advise him, he must learn the father role in a few short months. His confusion mounted, and he "p-h-h-h-h-ts."

Another runaway, Gretchen, shared her disappointment and anger toward physically abusive parents that motivated her to "keep running away from all my problems." From a rural region near the shelter, Gretchen was severely physically abused by both her father and mother. She ran away from home, leaving a brother behind. Her parents worked for a large national corporation—her mother was a service worker; her father worked on the factory floor. Tall and slight, this redhead revealed a deep confusion about how to meet the normal expectations of the daughter role in a healthy parent-child relationship: "Daughters should not physically strike their mothers." This is an obvious, or normal enough, expectation to hold, but for Gretchen, it became a sadly absurd impossibility. Gretchen's parents were abusing her physically, and she had to be disobedient in order to survive. Here she shared the dilemma of not wanting to hit her mother back, even when her mother was choking her:

> My mother beat me—but I'm not afraid of my mother! The last time she beat me up—I had respect—I did not hit her back until the day she got arrested. She was beating the shit out of me and I would not hit her back! I cried, I felt so sorry for myself, but I didn't hit her back! And she was choking me and she was cutting off my circulation, but I did not hit her back! The only thing I did was say, "Get the fuck off me!" and I called her a name, and that was it. When I tried calling the cops upstairs, she came up there, hanging up the phone and punching me! She went downstairs after she was done hitting me and yelled at me for an hour, saying, "Oh, you think you're all bad," and all this other stuff. Just kept yelling for about an hour! I totally can't talk to her. I'm so pissed off. . . . I've never really met anybody who's had as bad a story as I've ever had.

This traumatized sixteen-year-old carefully described her emotional struggle to live up to her side of the power bargain in the family—she won't "hit her mother back" and only "calls her a bad name." Meanwhile, her parents were abusing her and abusing the power that they have over her. Gretchen was battling out a moral stance with herself—whether to hit her mother back as her mother tried to strangle her! She reported crying and being "pissed off" at her before Gretchen finally decided to run away. However, Gretchen fought back against her inclination to strike her mother back. "Get the fuck off me!"—her angry runaway survival behavior won out in the end. Gretchen resolved this dilemma by initiating self-protective, but rebellious, behavior that consisted of running away. She confided that when she arrived at the shelter, she was "scared to death, but I kept telling myself, anything is better than being at home!"

"Being at home," for many young people, constituted being in the unbearable moral situation of living in a one-down power position to a person who was abusing them. Still, that person was their mother, father, or guardian—someone whom they were supposed to love and obey. Runaways struggled to conform to impossible norms: obeying abusive and incestuous parents and attempting to fulfill certain roles without having had any role-modeling. They reported that they loved their parents and, at the same time, were angry at their parents. Runaways struggled to reconcile these powerful and conflicting emotions. They had beliefs about how their families should be, but they saw how it really was. The emotions that this dissonance produced simmered under the surface of their family interactions and formed an intangible, but powerful, body of rage, which I will discuss in the next section.

RESSENTIMENT *AND EMOTIONAL CAPITAL*

Disappointment, indignation, and anger at perceived injustices were motivating factors in runaway behavior. German scholar Max Scheler (1961) observed a Nietzchean built-up anger that he termed (from the French) *ressentiment. Ressentiment* is a simmering anger that cannot be expressed openly because it is directed at someone or something that has power over the actor. Scheler's notions of *ressentiment* describe exactly the rage and indignation that animated the runaways' perspectives, which led to the development of another notion inspired by this investigation, "emotional capital."

I offer the idea of "emotional capital" to assist in conceptualizing a reserve of power for runaways who perceived themselves as under attack and drawing upon "something" that emboldened them. Although its fit is not perfect in all instances, the argument is useful in explaining an intangible resource I observed in runaways. Emotional capital consists of built-up *ressentiment* that formed when the young people were not able to safely or comfortably express their anger at being treated unjustly. They "stuffed" (sublimated) their feelings, but the feelings didn't go away. These submerged emotions readily surfaced as the youths recalled exchanges and interactions with dominating and severe authority figures. This "capital" formed a kind of empowered rage for the scared runaways. The emotion capital became, in effect, a symbolic resource for disempowered youths. When under attack, they could call up this indignant "attitude" and use it to power their runs and justify their behavior.

Perceiving that they were in subordinate powerless positions to authority, combined with being mistreated and feeling angry, created an unbearable time bomb of emotion that lead to explosive runaway situations for some adolescents. Many youths recounted vicious arguments culminating in defiant runaway behavior—many slammed out of doors and bolted through windows, leaving only with the clothes on their backs and rancor in their young hearts.

Gretchen articulated her rage in a concise and intense manner:

> I hate my father to death, and there's no way in hell anyone can make me go back there, or even get me to call, or even anything! I dislike my mother and my father. I've disliked them ever since I can remember—I've always hated them since I was two years old. I remember that two-by-four! It's something you don't forget, as if it was yesterday—you don't forget a two-by-four coming at your face—No, never, you never forget something like that. . . . I guess my father right now is looking for me; I've heard it from friends. He says to my friend's father, "The next time I see her, I'm going to shoot her," and this and that. I know my father wants to kill me! When I drove away in the cop car, he went shhhht, like that [indicates drawing her finger slowly across her neck as if to slit her throat]. The guy wants to kill me. . . . Whatever . . . [laugh]

Gretchen pointed to scars from the two-by-four blows as she recounted the incident. She had been holding on to the pain from this incident for fourteen years. She had plenty of new reasons to feed her fury—recent physical altercations. However, she focused her emotional work on recounting and remembering the injustices perpetrated upon her in her early life. German scholar Max Scheler describes this seething, built-up resentment:

> *Ressentiment* denotes an attitude which arises from a cumulative repression of feelings of hatred, revenge, envy, and the like

. . . . When a person is unable to release these feelings against the persons or groups evoking them, thus developing a sense of impotence, and when these feelings are continuously reexperienced over time, *ressentiment* arises. (Scheler, 1961, p. 24)

Ressentiment can only arise if these emotions are particularly powerful and yet must be suppressed because they are coupled with the feeling that one is unable to act them out—either because of weakness, physical or mental, or because of fear. Through its very origin, *ressentiment* is therefore chiefly confined to those who serve or are dominated at the moment, who fruitlessly resent the sting of authority. (Scheler, 1961, p. 48)

Normative expectations in family dynamics preclude giving teenagers completely equal voice in family regulations. However, in most families, negotiation and dialogue occur between parents and adolescents, and agreements are talked out and reshaped over time, as family members work out living arrangements that seem fair to all members of the household. However, runaways reported that in their families, negotiation and dialogue were not occurring. They told of walking in the door and getting into yelling matches and physical altercations. Runaway teens did not perceive their parents to be people with whom they could talk things out or share feelings and perceptions. Runaways believed that they were not "allowed" to direct their anger upward toward parents, police, teachers, social workers, all the adults who wielded power over them. They found that they were supposed to obey their elders and be dutiful children, or get rejected, yelled at, or struck physically. Respecting authority is a key expectation for young people to adhere to, but it is complicated in situations in which youths believe that authority is misused, severe, and too exacting. Scheler's *ressentiment* develops for teenagers who are victims of sexual and physical abuse, or for members of families that have stringent rules and inflexible parenting styles. The youths suppressed their feelings of rage and indignation because it was not "safe" for them to express their feelings, opinions, and ideas in their harsh family settings.

What is the "payoff" for runaways such as Gretchen to hold onto these old angers at unfairnesses committed by abusive parents? French thinker Pierre Bourdieu (1977) developed the notion of cultural reproduction called "cultural capital"—an intangible resource with its own economy. Although Bourdieu's cultural capital consists of a symbolic resource that is based on socioeconomic class status, transmitted culturally from parents to children, influences social skills, and ensures class reproduction (cultural transmission of social class "rules"), "emotional capital" is different. Rules about expressing emotion may vary depending on socioeconomic class status, but emotional capital is not exactly connected to social class or class reproduction.

Emotional capital is influenced by such factors as power, class, gender, and age. Emotions contain a dimension of power. People are a little afraid of other people when they express "strong feelings"—especially anger and hostile emotions that can lead to physical violence. But also, someone who shows their full fear, or love, or sadness can frighten the people around them. Free expression of passion contains an element of unleashed animalism or unharnessed nature. "Refined" people do not freely express their emotions. What is refined about them? Among other things, their emotions are under control and "in hand." Socioeconomic class and culture affect how people learn to express their emotions. Also, as people mature, age tends to tone down the full free expression of emotional capital.

Emotional capital is similar to cultural capital in that it forms a reserve for the people who have it to draw upon. People can let slip a comment about "the Guggenheim" at dinner and signal to all that they know of a beautiful building in a nice neighborhood in one of the greatest cities in the nation. We do not always use cultural, or emotional, capital—but it is there. Emotional capital is educational and cultural—but another kind of information is learned. It is built from surviving distressful situations, storing memories and judgments. Cultural capital forms a wisdom about the "refined and educated world"—emotion capital is often about a frightening "underworld." Instead of being shared during civilized dinner conversations, emotional capital is often evoked in surprising displays of angry passion. It is bravado, and it serves runaways well.

The feelings that runaways experience when they remember the anger, fear, and disappointment at the injustices committed against them form a symbolic resource of "emotional capital" that they can tap when feeling defenseless and disenfranchised.

Angry young teenagers with "bad attitudes" toward adults, such as police and parents whom they believe are overly restrictive, form a social cohort that can be seen on hip-hop videos and in living rooms across America. Disenfranchised young people—alienated from schools, jobless, living in families that are not meeting their emotional and social needs—draw on emotional capital when they express what they feel is righteous indignation over their perception that life is unfair for them. Their emotional capital forms a reserve of energetic passion that can be mobilized to empower these youths whom no one listens to, or takes seriously—until they runaway, commit a status offense, or commit a violent crime.

For runaways, emotional capital becomes a source of power when they feel particularly trapped and confused. Perceiving themselves as without a voice or agency and defenseless in impossible family dilemmas, runaways mobilized this resource in defensive moves to give them a sense that they "had something" to energize themselves into acting on their own behalf. They used this emotional capital when they would tell old stories and call up past victimizations—it manipulated adults, social service workers, and shelter counselors to feel sorry for them and obtain needed social services. In a sense, runaways cashed in the emotional capital and used it to get their survival needs met. Unlike cultural capital, though, emotional capital is not always a positive or pleasant resource to draw upon. Flaring bursts of rage can foster ruptures and conflict. Although breaks from abusive relationships might be necessary, and utilizing emotional capital to power the runs may facilitate them, using emotional capital resources can contain an element of destructiveness.

Denying hurt and fear, as if burying it deep inside, is another source of "stored" emotional resource. Putting aside the expression of hurt feelings, sadness, rejection, and also fear is necessary for a young person who has to act like a "toughie" to survive. They can't "afford" feelings of loss and confusion—they have to get about the business of running away, and then of survival—learning the skills of the street. Runaways first need to find the courage and power to run away—feelings of rage and fury are energizing. Street survival consists of an emotional immediacy of its own—there is no time to feel and heal. Runaways deny and bury hurt and fear because these feelings may make them feel, seem, and be vulnerable. In daring displays of "bad attitude," runaways allow only the expression of—"spend"—rage and anger.

One boy inadvertently described this notion of stored-up emotional capital as he explained his change of heart and his desire to turn his life around. This fifteen-year-old Puerto Rican gang member insisted that he had changed now, because if he hadn't changed, he would be feeling very differently. He carefully described how he would have drawn upon this "bad attitude" if he had needed to:

> I been here two or two and a half weeks, and a lot went through my head in these two and a half weeks. I swear on my mother—if I was like I used to be, I would a been like, "Fuck that! I do what I want to do! I ain't never gonna get off the street! Fuck everybody! Fuck this place!" I be back on the streets in two weeks—I don't care! But now my head is cleared out. I'll chill, get outta here, see my girl, and I'll never be part of this program again! (Carlos)

Carlos would have been drawing upon old *ressentiment* —"Fuck this! Fuck everybody!"—to power him through his experience in the public juvenile facility, if it weren't for the change of heart he reported experiencing. For some runaways, the emotional capital of resentment, rage, hurt, fear, and anger formed a "savings bank" of empowerment that they drew upon to guide them in the decision making and understanding of their lives. They harbor their resentments for later. Their stories of past failures in their interactions with their parents formed an arsenal of emotional weapons that they drew upon to protect themselves when they felt frustrated, disappointed, and hopeless.

Emotional capital is there for runaway teens, if they need it. Sometimes it appeared to be all they had—the only thing they drew upon for strength, to get a sense of themselves, and to make sense of their situation. Gretchen continued with her story:

> Everybody else's families are so much better than mine was. They sit down; they talk; they ask you, "How was work? How was your day? What did you do today in school? Where did you go? What did you do today and did you have fun?" My family's like, "Get your fuckin' ass down here and if you

don't, you're grounded!" And then they would hit you for no apparent reason—that's not how children should be raised. Little kids should be treated with respect; it only makes it worse when they're growing up. If you'd gotten beat up as long as I'd been beat up, after a while the pain doesn't matter! My father used to drag me down the stairs by my hair. One time my parents were fighting and my mom went upstairs and called the police, and my father dragged me down fourteen stairs by my hair! He just goes dragging me through the house by my hair! I'm definitely afraid of my father . . .

Here, this runaway clearly outlined a picture of her idea of a happy family that cares and communicates and then detailed the *ressentiment* that made her forswear ever attempting reattachment to her family by going back to her home of origin. The disappointment in "how it is" versus her understanding of "how it should be," however romanticized, was real to her. This disappointment, together with her fear and pent-up *ressentiment*, fueled her decision to run and never go back.

In summary, Scheler (1961) describes an anger that is inexpressible because it is felt by a subjugated person who "fruitlessly resents the sting of authority," but fears acting on it. This anger builds into a pool of held *ressentiment* that forms an arsenal of emotions that eventually can be called upon to empower the youths to run away from the unjust treatment of them by their parents. The emotional capital also helped the runaways make sense of their behavior. By calling up old anger or remembering past maltreatment, they bolstered their decisions to run and reminded themselves of the meaning of their disobedience. Notions of defiance and the politics of the aim of anger are discussed in the next sections, which shed further light on the central role of anger in runaway behavior.

RAGE AND INSUBORDINATION:
DEFIANT RUNNING AWAY

Philosopher Elizabeth Spelman articulates an important dimension in the relationship between anger and insubordination, unraveling the active connection between the feeling and the behavior:

Insofar as dominant groups wish to place limits on the kinds of emotional responses appropriate to those subordinate to them, they are attempting to exclude those subordinate to them from the category of moral agents. Hence there is a politics of emotion: the systematic denial of anger can be seen as a mechanism of subordination, and the existence and expression of anger as an act of insubordination. (1989, p. 270)

What makes Spelman's relationship between emotion (anger) and action (insubordination) intriguing is the injection of an analysis of the dynamics of power into the emotion-action equation. It can be usefully applied to illuminate a key configuration in the family—that of the authority of parent over child. For runaways, the authority was perceived as severe and unreasonable, dampening communication. For them, expression of anger necessarily became an act of insubordination because in their families, runaways reported that they felt they could not locate appropriate outlets for discussion and release of these feelings. In the intensely conflicted families of runaways, according to the youths, no safe avenue was freely provided to express anger in a "healthy," normative fashion. Anger itself became an act of subordination, even without the runaway behavior. Anger motivated the run, a much more concrete act of insubordination. Many of the runaways' accounts fit this description.

Some adults tend to deny teenagers the (Spelman's) status of "moral agents" perhaps, in part, because adults perceive youths as lacking adult experience and reasoning power. Runaways protest that their parents would not reason problems out with them or give them a voice in family affairs and regulations. Limiting acceptable emotional responses as inappropriate for teenagers includes denying them equal status, which reinforces their subordination. This produces benefits for parents and adults in other ways: parents limit their subordinate children's anger—and deny their moral agency—for three reasons.

First, if parents, police, and social service agents believe that young people do not have the capacity for moral reasoning, they may deny them any kind of status as "moral agent" and treat them arbitrarily as needing complete supervision. But, as Carlos said, "you grow up fast, especially on the streets." Although many runaways weren't experiencing the difficult lives on the streets that teenagers from more urban settings, like Carlos, were, the treachery of life inside a family in intense conflict affords many young people a glimpse of what Patricia Hill Collins calls the "outsider within" perspective: a wisdom that comes from being afforded a "distinct view of the contradictions between the dominant group's actions and ideologies" (Collins, 1991, p. 11). It is just this contradiction that runaways attempt to come to grips with in their ruminations, for example, "I would never hit my mother, but she was strangling me." The youths are confronted with both the pull of trying to meet the expectation of the family norms and the violation of those norms— all in the same interactions. However he or she resolved this dilemma, by running away or not, the young person may have gained valuable insight, experience, and reasoning power. But no matter to the adults, the subordinate adolescent was still denied moral agency, and his or her emotional response was limited from expressing any insight, angry or not.

The second problem in the "mechanism of subordination" lies within the assumption that young people do not have moral agency due to their youthful status. When adults and parents act on this assumption and continually disempower the adolescent, they create the very strain and tension that leads to runaway behavior. Disenfranchised, disbelieved, and cut off from the agency, autonomy, and expression that they seek, young people felt a growing frustration and resentment toward parents, adults, teachers, and police who, they believed, did not treat them with the respect they deserved. Excluding them from the table, as it were, adults tried to control this politics of emotion through controlling youths' anger— but this strategy backfired, often leading to even more explosive emotional expression by dominated youths.

Third, if Spelman's ideas of domination apply to parents as a dominant group, we could say that it benefits adults to perceive youths as powerless, weak, and dependent, with no experience and no ability to reason things out morally. Whose interests are served by limiting youths' rage and maintaining subordination of young people? Parents can "get away with" the mistreatment, abuse, and cruel inflexibility that they perpetrate while hiding behind the excuse that they are disciplining unruly children. Or, adults hide behind a notion that adolescents aren't really "people" whom parents have to treat with respect. In turn, children are "supposed" to withstand this abusive behavior without responding with anger and indignation because they are subordinate in the power dynamic and thus limited to "appropriate" emotional expression. Spelman cautions that "those who unjustly wield power and authority over others will be pleased if those they oppress find some way to censor their anger" (1989, p. 272). Young people have found a way to "censor their anger"—by struggling to faithfully adhere to normative expectations such as, "I would never hit my mother—even when she is strangling me." It is precisely when the youths defy these censoring moral devices and act on their own behalf that runaway behavior manifests.

One ninth grader's story illuminated this "normative expectation bind." She began her story by expressing her outrage at the Department of Social Service worker who told her that, in order for DSS to provide protection for her from her physically abusive parents, she would need to "go home and get physical evidence!" Red-haired Anne marched right into the interview, sat down, and began talking before a question was even asked. She jumped right in, explaining that she wasn't a bad person, or in trouble like the other youths, that she was here because her parents were "kicking the shit out of her." She wanted that to be clear:

> I'm not here 'cause I'm in trouble. I'm here with DSS 'cause—I'm not in trouble—'cause my parents need help. I'm not here 'cause I stole a car or 'cause I did any of these things that other people that are here have done. I'm here for help 'cause I can't stay at my house anymore. I was on the run, and I didn't go to school, and then I was talking to some people and they were like, "You know, you gotta—what are you gonna do? Run for the rest of your life, 'til your eighteen?" That's cool, you know—I'm going to be hiding out for the rest of my life! Hiding from the police, hiding from my parents! I have to get out of the country because if I stay here then the police will all know me—then I'll be on milk cartons and everything!
>
> I just—I don't want it to be that way, so I just said, "Well, what should I do?" And my friends are like, "Go to DSS!"

And I'm like, "No!" 'cause I heard that was a really bad thing. And DSS, I heard they screwed your life over bigger than it was already. And they did. They told me to go home and get physical evidence! That's what DSS told me, "Go home and get physical evidence!" Oh, OK, I'll go home and get the shit kicked out of me so you can have physical evidence! That's a good thing to do . . .

So I was on the run again—from everybody now, 'cause I was running from my parents, and from DSS, and from the police, and from everybody! So then one of my friends said, "So go home,"—she said, "Well, if DSS tells you to go home and get physical evidence, go home and get physical evidence for them!" And I was like, "No, I'm not putting up with it anymore!" So I went to the school psychologist and I told her what was going on, and I said that I'm not going home—I can't! I told her everything that has ever happened to me before in my whole life—well half, not even a fourth, of the things that ever happened to me in my whole life, but the recent things . . .

Anne used running away as a lifesaving strategy to escape repeated physical assaults. She was willing to listen to friends, DSS workers, and school psychologists—people who were her equals and people who had power over her—to help solve her conflict, but, full of mixed emotion toward her parents—anger and fear—she knew she had to stay away from their chaotic behavior. Anne described an altercation with her mother:

My mom said to me, "Come here, you asshole!" And I said, "Mom, don't call me that!" And she said, "You can just get your stuff and walk out that door—I don't care if I ever see you again!" So I said, "Fine!" And I went and I got all my stuff that I really needed, like a jacket, and I came out of my room. It was the middle of the coldest—I don't remember what month it was but it was really cold, like in the middle of one of those ice storms, and—she knocked everything out of my hands! She said, "If you go out that door, I'm going to kill you!" And I just said, "Mom, I'm leaving—Bye!" I got everything I could manage to pick up without going next to her because she kept kicking me whenever I went next to her! She walked away to go in the bathroom and I reached down to grab everything that was closest to me, and I ran out the door!

"So I said, 'Fine!' and went and got all my stuff"—Anne's hurt was turning to exasperation, and in an angry huff, she says, "Bye!" and "ran out the door." But not before, as Anne tells it, her mother threatened to kill her and kicked her. In the story, Anne carefully presented herself as calm—"Mom, don't call me that!" instead of yelling back and calling her mother a name. Telling this story, Anne talked a mile a minute. She spoke nonstop at a furious pace, as if she were still running in her thoughts, running from her mother's kicks, threats, and name-calling.

Anne was determined to hold onto her rage and remember these fights, so that she could ensure that she would never return out of a softhearted forgetfulness:

> I'm not going home. I know that for a fact—if they try to make me go home then I'll run away! I will get caught someday, and then they'll probably make me go home, but I've only got three years 'til I'm eighteen years old, and those three years could be spent in places like this, or in a foster home, or on the run—'cause I'm not going home! Those are my three options: shelter, foster home, or running. If DSS says, "Go home!"— I'm running! If DSS says they're sending me to a foster home, I'll go. I don't mind.

Anne exhibited an adult skill at reasoning out her plans for her future. In her thought processes, she revealed that she knew what she needed and had made plans how to achieve it. Carefully working out her alternatives and articulating them displayed the moral agency that Spelman's dominant groups deny subordinates by limiting their expression of powerless rage. Anne's emotional responses of hurt and anger were definitely frustrating to her mother. Calling Anne an "asshole" revealed that something was amiss with the mother's sense of self and her role as parent/adult/guide/nurturer.

The next account shows how the dominant figure needs the subordinate one to be limited emotionally in order to perpetrate the wrongs "in peace." Anne believed that her stepfather thought he could not only limit her emotional alternatives but "get away with" physical abuse as well. And she shows that, through her anger, she was overthrowing the domination:

> I've been abused since I was a little kid. Just because he's my stepfather, he thinks I'm not his real kid, so he can beat me up or anything and it won't matter, 'cause I'll love him 'cause my real father's not around! Since I have to depend on someone, it's going to be him.
>
> But it's not—I can depend on myself! My mom doesn't think I can depend on myself; my stepfather doesn't think so; my sisters don't even think so. So I'm going to prove them wrong. I'm just going to say, "No, that's wrong; I'm not putting up with it!" And if they say, "Oh yes, you are . . . " I've told my mom, and she's said that so many times. "I'm not putting up with that!"—"Oh yes, you are!" "No, I'm not, Mom—see ya!" I'm so sick of her saying that I have to put up with her, 'cause I don't! And I'm not gonna!

In the showdown with her mother over whether she would "put up with it," Anne had won this round. Defiant and determined, this fifteen-year-old runaway was going to define her own limitations, even if it meant going against powerful societal controls that hold young people in the family in the subordinate position. Explosive, but determined and defiant, she finally expressed her insubordination by running away.

Anger is inappropriately powerful for a subordinate person, according to Spelman. Runaways are hesitant with this feeling at first, and they censor and sublimate this strong emotion. In their accounts, they describe struggling against expression of rage until they can no longer "put up with it"—whatever abuse and domination they experience. Then, the fury often erupts into anger-motivated runaway behavior. Runaways expressed anger and defied the "proper" politics of emotion, claiming the moral agency that was their due by wresting it from the hands of whom they perceived to be domineering parents and insensitive police officers and social workers. The next section focuses on the uncharacteristic expression of anger by the weak toward the strong.

ANGER AND THE POLITICS OF AIM

Theorist Arlie Hochschild posits a hierarchy of expressing anger. Characteristically, anger flows from a person in power "down" toward a person with less power.[3] It is problematic to aim anger upward at those who have power over those in subordinate positions. Hochschild calls this the "politics of aim" and notes:

> There is a relation between the distribution of power and sanction on the one hand and the target of feeling and expression in social situations. . . . Under certain social conditions, anger, insofar as it is deflected at all from its "rightful" target, tends to be deflected "down" into relative power vacuums. Thus, anger is most likely to be aimed at people with less power, and least likely to be aimed at people with more power. . . . There are important conditions under which the "aim" of the bestowers is deflected up—for example, in cases of "rebellion." Then, the latent, rule-constrained envy of the subordinate attacks the institutional arrangements to avert it. (1975, pp. 294-296)

This notion of a politics of aim is useful when examining runaway behavior. Runaways report simmering rage and growing resentment. Sanctions exist against expressing anger toward their parents, police, social workers, and all adult members of society who have power over them and whom they perceive to be treating them unfairly. In addition to societal proscriptions to obey parents and respect the wishes of their elders, runaways report a sense of futility in their attempts to reason out with adults the problems, conflicts, and family dilemmas that they experience. Parents, police—all adults—occupy a "one-up" power position in society over teenagers. They are "above" young people because adults govern youths and have all the power over them. Youths are often the recipients of the anger and abuse of their parents, consonant with Hochschild's hierarchical reasoning, but strong symbolic restraints keep young people from expressing anger back. However, teenagers do "strike back" and return the rage. When adolescents say, "I'm outta here!" and run away from home, they are aiming their anger and resentment uncharacteristically upward at authority:

If they do try to send me home, that's just going to be harder for me, and harder for the police, and harder for them! Some-day—I'm not saying they won't find me. They'll probably find me wherever I go, but then when they do, I'll run away some more. It would be so easy for me to run away from here. Not really so easy, but I could say I'm going over to the barn, and walk out the door and take off. I'm not saying I'm going to . . . but it would be so easy, and if they send me to another place like this. . . . Of course, running away—they'll send me to lockup or juvenile hall because I'm running away. But see, since I went to them first, I think they'll send me to a shelter because I went to them—told them that I was in danger and then if they'd make me go home, then I'd run away—and they made me go home! It's not like running—I warned them! (Anne)

Anne fine-tuned her definition of running away, careful not to upset the balance of anger and "aim" with the shelter staff. It was important to her definition of self to distinguish herself from youth offenders and delinquency. She insisted that she was running from abuse; crimes are committed against her, not vice versa. Anne wanted us to believe that she was not aiming her anger upward. She wanted her identity as an independent agent to be clear—she warned that she would run away and why. It was as if she didn't want to upset the status quo and give the impression that she was challenging the hierarchy of anger by aiming upward. She was clear with herself morally and wanted to be clear with us about it. Be-cause she went to DSS, and she called the school psychologist before running, she saw that as different than "kids who steal cars" and run away—"it's not like running—I warned them," she noted. She wanted to be involved in the definition and labeling of her behavior, the disposition of her whereabouts. She wanted to be in control of her life, without threatening the politics of aim:

My mom doesn't think it's bad for me; she thinks she's disci-plining me! It's not discipline, because when somebody doesn't do something wrong—I can remember so many times when I didn't do anything wrong! Like the other day, I was getting out of the shower—I was—I just got out of the shower! I was walking toward my bedroom and she said, "Get out of my way!" and she started kicking the shit out of me for no reason! I was just like . . . I didn't hit her back that time. But then the second time, after I got home from school that day and she did it again—I did hit her back because I was just like, "Mom, I'm not taking it!" And she was surprised that I hit her back! She stopped for a while. Then she started back in, and for the first couple times, I didn't hit her back. Then, when she got into it again, I hit her back—and she said, "It's disrespectful to hit your mom!" And I said, "No, it's not—it's disrespectful to hit your kid too! You hit your kid, you expect them to hit you back!" Especially my age, I can see her hitting my little three-year-old sister, saying, "Don't do that!" But my age—fifteen years old! You don't go smacking your kid around, saying, "Don't do that!" and they didn't do anything wrong! I can imagine if I ran up behind her and kicked her or something and she turned around and smacked me, but that's not what happened!

Anne clearly laid out her moral struggle over whether it was fair to strike back at her mother, and she expressed the hurt and rage at her mother's physical assaults, mixed with feelings of indignation. Indignation and outrage is anger that stems from believing you have been treated unjustly (Calhoun and Solomon, 1984, p. 306). If not diffused, it can build into Scheler's (1961) *ressentiment*.

Anne described two scenarios in which her mother could possibly be justified in striking her. One was if Anne had come up from behind her mother and "kicked her," and the other, if Anne were three years old and needed to be told, "Don't do that!" This was moral reasoning at its best by a wise and mature fifteen year old. Anne showed her understanding of the hierarchy of anger—a parent has the "right" to kick back at an incorrigible youth or to discipline a child. Although Anne struggled to understand and excuse the inappropriate behavior of her parent, she knew that she could not return to her family's care. She hung onto rage and moral reasoning to empower her to stay away from that physically and emotionally abusive situation. Her emotional decisions and reasoning were her symbolic resources that fueled her ability to stay morally intact, and to stay out of her mother's home. Anne attempted to avoid challenging the power framework of the politics of aim by leaving her home situation. Anne did not see herself as behaving inappropriately: "I was only getting out of the shower." "I didn't hit her back."

Anger is often fueled by the belief that someone has wronged you (Bedford, 1984, p. 277). Children's anger at their parents is complicated because these adults are supposed to provide food, shelter, love, approval, sense of self-worth—all the components that help nurture children into adulthood—and these are the same adults who wrong them. *Ressentiment* encompasses this dimension of anger, of not being able to express anger "safely" because the person experiencing it is in a "one-down" power position, subordinate to an authority figure. The politics of aim comes into play because of the sanctions against expressing anger toward one's elders and other adults in power. However, runaways did express their anger upward in defiance of this sanction. Anne felt powerless and subordinate in her life—under the authority of her parents, the police, the Department of Social Services workers, the school psychologist. Determined not to return home, her anger and *ressentiment* guided her to form a defiant plan of action that included "keeping on running for three years," thereby defying the politics of the aim of anger.

CONCLUSION

This chapter explored how the position of young people in society affects their emotional motivations. Using a conflict perspective, which holds that all interactions and events between members of society are guided by struggles over material and symbolic resources, I examined the power dynamics in the structures of runaways' lives.

I began by looking at the regulatory rules and sanctions that structure the movement of young people. I described their subordinate position in many, if not all, social structures. I presented examples from interviews that convey the youths' impressions that much of the domination they live under is unjust, unfair, and overly arbitrary. I explored the youths' struggles over their desire to conform to healthy normative expectations of social structures, such as the family, schools, and legal community, and their experiences of unjust and nonnormative treatment in these structures, such as parental physical and sexual abuse or insensitive instructors or police officers. Such struggles produced an emotional tension that guided their decisions to run away—their means to alleviate this tension. Runaways' stories showed that running away is a rebellious response to powerlessness, motivated by their feelings of anger, resentment, and disappointment as they interacted with their families, at school, with police, and with social service workers. Whether we view the youths as hoods or heroes, using the sociology of emotion fleshes out pictures of their situations as full of complexities and challenges that adults must face and resolve.

Runaways report that adults set too many unfair regulations. That they tried to follow all the rules and not break laws—even rules and laws they didn't believe were fair—produced confused emotional struggles that often led to outbreaks of anger. Unable to express their anger and frustration because of their subordinate power position within the family, they sometimes developed what Max Scheler (1961) calls *ressentiment*—a simmering anger that cannot be directly expressed. I argued that many of the confused feelings of rage, fear, and resentment could slowly form a kind of "emotional capital" that the youths would draw upon to fuel their angry, defiant runs. Loosely paralleling Pierre Bourdieu's (1977) ideas about cultural capital, I presented the thesis that "emotional capital" is a symbolic resource for otherwise disenfranchised, disbelieved, and maltreated youths. For some runaways, their backs are against the wall—they have no where to turn, no one to turn to, no resources to mobilize on their behalf. All they have is this tough, angry attitude of resentment and stored-up memories of being abused and misunderstood. Like an emotional arsenal, they draw on these feelings to empower them with the anger and self-righteousness they need to effect an escape from unacceptable conditions.

I argued that Spelman's (1989) philosophy, which links anger (feeling) and insubordination (behavior), is useful in understanding runaways' accounts. Runaways are placed in powerless positions in the family. For runaways, anger itself is insubordination, and expressing those angry feelings by running away especially challenges the politics of emotion in the family power struggle. Aiming anger "upward" toward parents, police, and other adults represents one aspect of Hochschild's (1975) theory of the politics of aim as it relates to the runaway problem. Anger flows naturally downward in the hierarchy of power—from those in dominant positions toward those who are subordinate. For a runaway teen to be angry, to yell, to physically strike, or to run away from parents and adults is "uncharacteristic" within the framework of Hochschild's theory, except in cases of "rebellion." Using the sociology of emotion and a conflict perspective when evaluating the stories of adolescent runaways reveals patterns of rebellion against perceived maltreatment, whether we judge any individual youth to be delinquent or brave in their actions.

Night Flight

I step into darkness
Cuz the light is just too bright.
My arms are open wide
As I commence my flight.
My hair flows like the wind while I rise above this earth.
All I trip off
All that gives me grief
All that makes me cry
All that FUCKIN BULLSHIT
Gets clearer as I fly.

Ain't no crack fiends in my sky
No hospital IV's and wondering, "What is it I got?"
No infections
No cousins getting shot
No stressed friends
No man troubles
No lack of ends
No asshole roommates
And no tears.

Up here I shine like the SUN
And I'm mysteriously beautiful like the moon.
This is my therapy
I can descend soon
Cuz during my Night Flight
Life is All Right.

Martha Torres-McKay

Chapter 5

Broken Hearts and "Bad Attitudes"

There's that thing where if you really want to run—I don't know—that's what I felt when I ran the first time. I never thought I could do it; I never thought I could runaway. But every time after that, it's—easy. You could do it all the time . . . I was running, running away from all my problems and they'd never catch up with me! But they will—now I realize that. It's not what I thought. [Reflecting on running away.]

Gretchen, age sixteen

INTRODUCTION: THEORETICAL OBSERVATIONS

Some popular myths about teenage runaways include thinking of them as disobedient juvenile delinquents who have no respect for authority, as psychopathological children in need of therapy, or as adventuresome pleasure seekers. By drawing on different perspectives in sociology, the interactionist and conflict viewpoints, and a theory of deviance—the social bond theory—and by using a sociology of emotion to examine the emotional narratives of the runaways' stories, I have shown runaway behavior in a different light.

There is wide debate over the state of the American family and whether that institution is on the decline (Popenoe, 1988; Bumpass, 1990; Cheal, 1991). It may appear that once adolescent children leave—or are forced out of—their families or their homes, no means exists to heal or repair these breaches of trust. However, by talking to young people and listening to their hopes for reconciliation, one can see that possibilities for healing abound.

139

Family arrangements are in dynamic motion. At the same time that we see the hopeful growth of different family arrangements, such as households headed by same-sex partners and binuclear, blended families, we also witness the tragic developments of home-less families and throwaway children. As we listen to sons and daughters talk about their struggles to enact covenance and protec-tion in their lives, we see the emotional and moral dimensions of their new definitions of "family."

Runaways Do Not **Want** *to Leave Home*

The emotional dilemma over the decision to run away is created by the desire to stay home and the need to be safe. Runaways search for methods by which they can meet their families' expectations. The problem is that these youths come from families in extreme conflict. They try to continue to love their parents even when their parents are abusive, they struggle with not hitting their parents back when their parents physically abuse them, and they incorporate experiences of familial sexual abuse into their lives as best they can. Runaways report chronic and acute malfunctioning in their families—physical and sexual abuse, authoritarian and arbitrary parenting styles, neglect and abandonment, and other forms of unreasonable and unsolvable family conflict. All these family issues and events cause emotional deliberations and evoke expressions of confusion that reflect their moral dilemma. Runaways struggle to conform and comply with rules and regulations they believe to be unfair and arbitrary. They struggle to comply, but ultimately, runaways felt that they had to defy the normative proscriptions of family unity in order to survive their crises. Their emotional struggles are caused by crises of trust, and I argued that runaways wrestle with their dilemmas because, ideally, they do not want to leave home.

Running Away Is a Search for Connection

Running away from home, paradoxically, is a search for connec-tion—connection to "safe" (not abusive or arbitrary) authority. The emotional connections that Hirschi (1985) terms "social bonds" are powerful directives full of expectations that signal families to form social structures within which children are nurtured, protected, and socialized. Brennan, Huizinga, and Elliott's (1978) explanatory theory of runaway behavior encompasses this key observation of the strength and role of the social bond in human behavior. O'Neill's (1994) covenant theory is also applicable in the runaway case. Children need love and guidance in supportive environments to make the transition from adolescence to healthy adulthood. When parents cannot provide for children's and adolescents' needs—or instead meet them with abuse and neglect—the emotional, moral, and social bonds that hold the family together weaken, become ineffectual, and can rupture. While on the run, runaways then seek reattachment and protection—preferably, reattachment with the family or, possibly, attachment with peers, in school, or in community agencies. Being on the run evolves into a continual search for sources (peers, police, community agencies, foster homes, and juvenile placement facilities) of protection and the means to meet their needs for attachment and connection.

Running Away Is Emotional and Often Fueled by "Emotional Capital"

Theories of emotion suggest that running away is often inspired by angry feelings of resentment in young people who perceive their powerless position in society as being unfair. These strong feelings empower them to move away from the inequity and maltreatment in their families and foster care placements. Drawing from Bourdieu's (1977) ideas about cultural capital, I proposed that runaways' feelings constitute an "emotional capital" that forms an arsenal of "bad attitude," backed by simmering *ressentiment* and victim memories, which runaways draw upon to make sense of why they have to leave home. This "capital" forms a symbolic resource for youths, as they leave home, fearful and full of rage, with not much more than bad memories of unfair and abusive interactions. They "cash" in this emotional reserve, calling forth outbursts of rage and fury as they remember their experiences—their emotional capital fuels them in their decisions to run. Drawing on stored emotional capital helps give meaning to their disobedience: with a reserve of anger, resentment, or hurt feelings, they justify finding themselves in shelters, police stations, and out on the streets. Runaways trade in this "capital" when telling their stories to one another and to Social Services workers, manipulating others into feeling sorry for them and meeting their needs. Emotional capital consists of stored-up reserves of emotional memories, derived from denying the horrors of abuse and stuffing rage over perceptions of injustice, and may surface at a later time, if needed. I have suggested that this emotional capital is a kind of cultural capital that runaways revealed when telling how they came to be in the shelter and how they felt about their life experiences.

Running Away Is Insubordination and Rebellion

Runaways' stories chronicle the difficult emotional struggles out of which they decide to overthrow powerful proscriptive social bonds. The disruptive emotional chaos in which they leave their families and other social settings led me to conceive of running away as a rebellious act. Spelman's (1989) philosophy of anger and insubordination includes the idea that people in the dominant position wish to limit people in the subordinate position from feeling certain emotions such as anger. Subsequently, anger itself is conceptualized as insubordination. Drawing on this philosophy, I argued that running away is a power struggle between adolescents and adults that includes this dynamic of angry insubordination. Running away is insubordinate because adolescents are in dominated "one-down" power positions in their families and in the other social structures they inhabit. Hochschild's (1975) ideas about the politics of the aim of anger show that the anger which spawns the runaway act is uncharacteristically pointed "upward" toward parents and adults. Anger flows "safely" downward in the hierarchy of power—from boss to worker, from parent to child. When runaways express anger toward adults—strike back, run away—they upset the etiquette of their limited, subjugated position. I have shown that this politics of the aim of anger illuminates a central aspect of anger in defiant runaway behavior.

Thus, applying the ideas from the sociology of emotion to social bond theory and conflict theory, I argued that we can view runaway behavior as serving a twofold purpose for adolescents. First, the formation of "emotional capital"—composed of feelings such as anger, hurt, disappointment, loss, *ressentiment,* and indignation—ultimately provides runaways with emotional and moral strength to overthrow the proscriptions to stay home and be loyal to the family. Even an abusive, nonfunctioning family is difficult to leave, and these strong submerged emotions fuel runaways' escapes from perceived maltreatment, unfair arbitrary regulations, or physical/sexual abuse at home. The runaway aims anger "upward" at those in power and thus defies the social expectations in the family. The social bond in families in severe conflict is a noose for the adolescent, instead of a gentle lifeline, and emotion motivates the adolescent to commit the ultimate insubordination—running away.

Second, applying social bond theory to the runaway experience, I argued that running away from home becomes a search for connection—either to attempt rapprochement with the family of origin or to seek protection and attachment with peers or in another community agency. As Scheff notes, the "maintenance of bonds is the most crucial human motive," and adolescents seek connections while on the run (1990, p. 3). The sociology of emotion illuminates the fluid and dynamic character of the social bonds in families, among peers, and in community relations. By studying the emotional characteristics of the runaways' stories, I argued that social bonds can be seen to weaken, strengthen, rupture, and heal.

This last observation, that of the healing and revitalization of the emotional connections in the families, and with other social sources, is most intriguing for the runaway situation. That the emotional, moral, and social connections that hold the runaways in alliance with society can change, improve, and repair speaks to the presence of resiliency in our human interactions. This resourcefulness of spirit is one which runaways can draw upon and which society can use to offer them help, to find hopeful outcomes to what may be considerably disadvantaged beginnings.

RUNAWAYS' RECOMMENDATIONS

The search for social policy solutions guides much of the research on the topic of teenage runaways. In an article from a social policy journal, one theorist uses insights from her literature review to develop several alluring policy recommendations, including encouraging supportive communities for teens, especially teen moms, building school programs, especially programs that are sensitive to runaways who continue in school while on the run, and allotting more staff time for children who are first entering shelters and youth residential programs (Appathurai, 1991). Another youth theorist advocates a "community youth charter":

> The adolescent experience is not a collection of isolated experiences; rather it is an organization of experiences and exposures in the various social worlds of the community. Programs for adolescents should grow out of a community youth charter which promulgates the expectations and standards which can meet the developmental needs of the adolescents in the specific community. (Ianni, 1989, p. 279)

Ianni's youth charter would link different community agencies to respond to adolescent (including runaway) needs.

During the interviews and in informal conversations, runaway teens had much to say about social policy and how they think the world should be set up. I will present teenage runaways' comments and let them speak directly about what they believe should be done. The ideas from the sociology of emotion, the search for connection, and running away as defiant rebellion remain apparent as themes, even throughout the runaways' comments and their opinions of society, and in their hopes and dreams for the future.

Schools: Less Is More, More or Less . . .

> What about school? I don't know. It's not really a good school, we don't really . . . it's not really worth that much! [laugh] I'm in tenth grade and I was in all honor's classes and everything, and it's just pretty much—just school, 'cause they're pretty bad. I live in a small town, but there's too much drugs, you know, and too much abuse in the town. It's just a dead end— anybody that gets into alcohol—they have a hard time gettin' out of that and staying in school. (Eva)

> I don't like to go to school. I'd like it if it were a little bit less—just three hours a day. We have it here [at the shelter]. If school was just three hours a day, it wouldn't be so bad! If school was just three hours a day, I would be happy—and I hate

math! It's not that I don't know how to do it; I just don't like it. It's a boring subject. I like science a lot! (Evander)

Oh man! I want a foster home outside of Hartford or anywhere around it—I don't want a foster home in the Flats because people are getting killed there with guns and knives! I've been fighting my whole life, and I'm done fighting. I just want to go to school with different people where I can get a good education and learn, and just start different, fresh, permanently! I don't want you to snatch it away from me! And if I get in trouble, I promise you: I will face the consequences—anything! I don't ask for much—all I ask for is a good school! (Isaiah)

Social Workers: Mixed Reviews, but They Do Give You a "Voice"

My DSS worker is an asshole. DSS workers—the way I look at it—they're supposed to be helping you, to take care of you, to help you bring out your problems, and all she does is cause problems. (Jimmy)

I'm in therapy at DSS. (I'm not DYS—DYS kids steal cars.) Three years ago I did counseling when I was at a foster home . . . . Whatever. . . . I went away for a year and came back to the foster home again. In order to move back home, I had to go to counseling. My counselor is nice; she wanted me to come here [to the shelter]. She helps me sort things out. My life was, like, crazy, and I was trying to figure out what I was going to do. I needed to find a place to live; I needed to find a job. Counseling, I mean, I knew in my head I was going to do it. I had it all sorted out in my head that I was going to go to counseling. But I felt that I was just wasting an hour of my time where I could be out job hunting or something. I'll go to counseling if these people [the shelter administrators] want me to go to counseling. Hell, I'll call George [her boyfriend], "Hey, meet me at my counselor's!" (Kate)[1]

I talked to a counselor—I don't like talking to—I'm not used to talking to people about this, and I've been bringing up a lot of stuff. But I don't like sitting down and talking to people about it because we've had some family counseling about it, and they just brought up more problems and made me want to run away more and more and more. (Gretchen)

Runaways have to deal with sexual harassment. You need to speak up about it [to your DSS worker or your counselor]. The more you run, the less they understand what's really going on. They just think I'm running away for the hell of it! I mean I realized that it's not going to do any good to keep running and hiding. I just figure if I get a chance to tell people—that will let the system do its job. It should be doing its job, but not if you don't tell 'em! I guess it means that I'm really taking responsibility for myself, realizing I'm not a little kid anymore, and I think it's time that I start growing up for myself. I realized that I'm big enough to take care of myself—I could take care of myself, if they were to set me somewhere and give me a house! I'd be able to pay for it. I'm a hard-working person! I feel that I'm way more mature—I've met plenty of fifteen-year-old girls—I can tell! (Gretchen)

Give Me a Good Foster Home

Yeah, basically I want to be put in a foster home in Eastbury, but I don't think they'll put me in a foster home there. I don't do much wrong. I get good grades in school, and I'm into a lot of sports and on yearbook and peer leadership and all kinds of things at my school. I promise I'll go to school and get good grades—just give me a chance. I'd stay in Eastbury and I'd get good grades, and my boyfriend's there, all my friends are there, and my school is there. It's true—my mom probably saw I was going to be getting in trouble and now I'm paying the consequences of it! They're probably going to give me something like community service, but that's OK because I'd do that anyway. I work at the Y and the Boys and Girls Club and all that so. . . . I'm sorry that I was in a stolen car. I don't like it here, but I did it, and now I have to pay for doing it. I can say I'm sorry, but that's not going to get me home. My mom's not going to forgive my boyfriend for getting me in trouble. (Amy)

Runaways' recommendations do not diverge far from the recommendations of policy analysts in this field. As Mesa-Bains and Barajas Dallas suggest in a report on dropout prevention:

> Students learn in many different ways and at different speeds. A student's academic level and ability and how the school treats the student in relation to it are key factors in determining whether a student will be successful and complete school. Learning handicaps, language difficulties, poor reading and math ability, suspension and retention are significant indicators that a student may drop out. (1986, p. 55)

Runaways told of their frustrations with math skills, language barriers, and the boredom and loss of interest due to being ahead of the remedial classes that they were placed in because of their poor attendance records. Their reports on social workers are mixed, often showing resentment at the power that social workers wield over them, and almost every runaway dreams of a "good foster home." However, the main point many runaways wanted to make was that they believed, however unrealistic it seems to others, that they could "make it," if given a chance to be independent.

Independence: "I Can Make It On My Own"

Running away from home for teenagers is a rebellious response to powerlessness, motivated by feelings of anger, resentment, and disappointment. Their solutions, time and again, were twofold: first, to escape the physical and sexual abuse, if any, the overly strict rules and arbitrary regulations, or the unbearable family conflicts; second, to seek safe haven to begin a life on their own in which they could flourish. Yearning for independence was a theme song for many of the runaways. They wanted to make their own decisions and face their own consequences. In many ways, they expressed their desire for independence, even if they often didn't display their ability to do so in law-abiding ways (by subsequently getting in trouble for fighting, selling drugs, and stealing cars). Yet they believed that getting out from under the arbitrary rules of unjust adults was the path to freedom:

> I and my mom were—we became close—and then I grew up and I decided that I need to be by myself. I don't—I want to live on my own. I would love to live on my own, but unfortunately, there's no state that's going to say I can live on my own. I always think that I would be so much better off by myself than living with my mom. (Amy)

> My best dream to come true would be walkin' outta here and bein' twenty-one years old! Just get a job and an apartment and get my life and just be able to do it! (Eva)

> I wanna be on my own. I wanna be a writer, a poet, a children's story writer, a Department of Social Service worker—but I would do it right! I would stick with one kid. I wouldn't let them switch DSS workers every two weeks. I would follow through the whole thing with each kid. I would try to get it as perfect as possible as they wanted it! If they wanted a home in South Westbury, I would make people be foster parents just to get my kid a home! I wanna good foster home, or be on my own! (Jean)

> I want my own apartment and I want to live there with Anne, Eric, Jesse, Gretchen, and Zackary! Let's go now, man! I can't wait for college! But I don't know if I want to go to college. I want to travel, too—like Ohio state. I want to go to Alaska! I don't know—do they have college in Alaska? (Michael)

> On the thirty-first I go to court. I don't know what they are going to do with me. I don't wanna go to lockup. I don't wanna go to some old lady foster home. I don't wanna go to the Flats 'cause . . . well . . . the girls don't like me but the boys take care of me. They always ask, "You got somewhere to stay tonight?" (Chabela)

How much of this was a "natural" longing for independence that occurs at the age of adolescence, and how much was the well-thought-out reasoning of mature young adults was unclear. Staying in their chaotic homes is certainly not indicated. Runaways were clear that they think that if they can get away from their abusive or overly strict parents, or ineffectual school situations, or specific social workers, or into a "good foster home," that resentment and anger would recede, that they would not need to utilize insubordination and spend emotional capital, that the politics of anger would become obsolete as a survival technique for them. Their recommendations and desires for independence indicated that they were aware of the contradictory expectations with which they struggled, and would have liked to bring their accomplishments in line with their goals.

As one sad, but determined, runaway visualized his future, he hoped for more than just independence. He envisioned love, support, honesty, communication, family, and happiness:

> I just want a foster family who are not scared to speak their mind, not holding back things until they just make me feel low. I want somebody to support me—to come to all my football games! And I want somebody to really, really, really—when I bring home anything from school, like report cards or notices or notes—everything—I want someone to really look at it and credit me! I want to get out of this system, just grow up, marry Kelly, go to the Marines for a couple years, take care of my family, get old, and die! (Isaiah)

We hope you make it, Isaiah.

CONCLUSION

What do runaways want? They protest if there is too much structure, and then claim they have been neglected and abandoned. They complain of too many rules and not enough freedom. Adults must strike the balance because, as Janus and colleagues suggest, "adolescence is a task of parenting," not solely a developmental stage for young people to get from childhood to adulthood (1987, p. 24). Parenting is teaching the art of negotiation and compromise. It is my contention that because the social, emotional, and moral bonds between runaways and adults are changeable and fluid, it is possible to envision adult intervention that would vitalize weakening emotional connections. It is imperative to further note, however, that the social interactions between runaways and adults are not equal exchanges—police, parents, and social workers have more power in society, power directly over the lives of runaways, and thus more responsibility for providing ways for teenage runaways to exercise their budding independence in normative ways and for providing safe locations for runaways to become connected and invested in their communities.

Notes

Chapter 1

1. Except for gender and racial/ethnic designations, all names and identifying characteristics, including age and geographic locations have been altered to protect participants' confidentiality.

2. "Throwaway" or "pushout" are terms coined by social service agencies in the 1980s. They refer to children who are abandoned or are kicked out of their parents' homes. This is a new category to consider when counting homeless and runaway youths.

3. Numbers and demographic data on homeless families and young people obscure the nature of the "new" runaway—many teens do not actually have a home to run from. A recent national survey dismally notes that 11 percent of the youths surveyed reported that they were homeless and living on the streets before arriving at runaway shelters (NASW, 1993, p. 1). Many runaways have no family inquiring after them. Instead, they have bolted from foster care settings or group homes and are only names on a buried police report. Over one-third of runaway youths come to homeless shelters from foster care homes (NASW, 1993, pp. 1-2).

4. Libertoff, 1980; Wilkinson, 1988; and Wells and Sandhu, 1986 provide excellent and thorough presentations of the history of running away in America, from which the main ideas in this summary are distilled.

5. Even as much youth activity was touted as alarming and dangerous, in 1974, Congress still enacted the Runaway Act, decriminalizing status offenses such as running away, reflecting the liberal social reformist attitudes that prevailed in the 1960s and 1970s. Police had to stop locking up runaways in secure facilities.

6. I am indebted to Brennan and colleagues, 1978, for this invaluable framework.

7. Another study notes that the major reason for remaining on the street is youths' perceptions that conflict within the family cannot be resolved. These teens have chosen to develop their own family from other street people rather than risk further rejection (Holdaway and Ray, 1992, p. 307). See also Wilkinson, 1987; Roberts, 1982; Adams, Gullota, and Clancy, 1985.

8. Today, the "runaway reaction" is considered to be a component of a personal conduct disorder (undersocialized nonaggressive) (Janus et al., 1987, p. 42).

9. A "nonfunctioning family" refers to a family with intense internal conflict. Physical and sexual abuse may be occurring, the family may lack open commu-

nications, it may have authoritarian parenting styles, or it may consist of neglectful, ineffectual, absent parenting.

10. This is a compelling argument, but it doesn't go deep enough. It does not suffice to say, "Society is going to hell in a handbasket," and argue for a return to "traditional" (mythical) values. In Chapter 4, a discussion of the power inequities that youths experience in relating to other people in the social structures they inhabit speaks to key aspects in the "blame the family" approach.

11. See Brennan and colleagues for an interesting presentation of how social class influences the causes of runaway behavior. For example, they develop a taxonomic description of runaways by whether they are boys or girls, delinquent or nondelinquent, middle or lower class, and alienated and rejected or "normal" (not displaying psychological problems). For example, one category is middle-class girls who are not delinquent. Although some of each type predominate in several groups, socioeconomic class does not play an overwhelming role in explaining the cause or source of runaway behavior in general (Brennan, Huizinga, and Elliott, 1978, pp. 294-297).

12. Ironically, narrowing the focus to a microanalysis of runaways uncovers an understanding of runaways on macrostructural levels.

13. In the course of this research, two adults identified themselves to me as "adult runaways" and agreed to interviews.

14. The two adult participants in this study, included in the overall sample percentages, were both female, white (one identified herself as Jewish American), and both in their thirties.

15. The USGAO combined Latino and other to include 13 percent (so the radical/ethnic breakdown from that report is 70 percent white, 17 percent African American, and 13 percent other).

16. This is my sample as compared to the national estimates discussed previously in this chapter.

17. In that report, "urban states" refers to states with the highest percent of their population living in urban areas, according to the 1980 census, and "rural states" are those with the lowest percentages living in urban areas. Although Massachusetts is considered an urban state, surrounding Vermont, Maine, and New Hampshire are not. The ten urban states were listed as California, New Jersey, Rhode Island, Hawaii, Nevada, New York, Utah, Florida, Massachusetts, and Arizona. The ten rural states were listed as Vermont, West Virginia, South Dakota, Mississippi, Maine, North Carolina, North Dakota, Kentucky, Arkansas, and New Hampshire. According to these divisions, most of the participants in this study would be considered "urban youths" if they were from the state of Massachusetts. I have, however, further distinguished between youths from nearby cities, such as Springfield, Massachusetts, or Hartford, Connecticut, for example, and youths from rural towns throughout New England. For example, if I refer to a youth as "urban," he or she is from a nearby city.

18. Ritual abuse is emerging as a contemporary phenomenon that has only recently begun to be reported. (There is some discussion as to whether it even exists or not.) It reportedly consists of atrocities committed against children in the

course of living in cult settings, with the children being forced to participate in cult ceremonies and initiations. The atrocities, and the depth of their evil, are difficult to imagine or believe. Children witness removal of human body parts and animal and human murders. Ritual abuse can involve physical and sexual violations of the children and forcing children to participate actively in the rituals.

19. According to one study, 46 percent of runaways had two parents in the homes from which they ran. This belies a common misconception that a great majority of runaways come from "broken homes." However, that study did note a connection between physical abuse and financial distress in the family (Janus et al., 1987, p. 40). As of 1988, 23 percent of American families with children under eighteen were single-parent families (Glick, 1994, p. 97).

20. Of the sample for this study, 19 percent reported running away from foster families or juvenile facilities.

21. In this study, runaways repeatedly related instances of being made to do more than their share of housework, of overly strict restrictions put upon them, or of other kinds of unfavorable treatment while living in foster care. One youth told me he thought that his foster mother was just "in it for the money—she didn't give a shit about me" (Isaiah).

Chapter 3

1. CHINS is a state Department of Social Services acronym for "Child in Need of Services." Parents and adults can request help through this program. The request can result in "protective custody" for the child in a locked-down "correctional" facility.

2. A "forming" or "building" of the bond differs from a "repair" of the bond. For instance, as a runaway makes a friend at the shelter or a crack house, I call this "building" an emotional connection. However, when a runaway forgives a sibling for past wrongs, and he or she discovers and nurtures an alliance in the family, I term this "repairing" of the bond. A bond may be constructed or created among strangers; it can only be repaired if it already existed.

3. As noted in Chapter 1, all the names and identifying characteristics of the participants, their exact locations, and their stories, except for gender and racial/ethnic designations, have been altered slightly to protect their privacy.

4. Emotional literacy is a term coined by writer and psychotherapist Claude Steiner to describe the skill gained from knowing about one's feelings—what they are, how to express them safely. It is the "capacity to understand and deal with emotion" (1986, p. 112). Steiner notes, "To be emotionally literate we need not only to feel, but to know. We need to know both what it is that we are feeling and what the causes for our feelings are. It is not sufficient to know that we are angry, guilty, happy, or in love. We also need to know the origin of our anger, what causes our guilt, why we are in love" (1986, pp. 116-117).

5. In this study, the sexual name-calling for the girls appeared as a particularly gendered phenomenon in the runaway experience: none of the boys reported that their parents called them names that were connected to their sexuality, sexual

identity, sexual experiences, or sexual behavior. None of the participants revealed their homosexuality outright, so issues of gay and lesbian sexual identity did not emerge for these adolescents, although 7 percent of runaways in shelters across the nation stated that they were forced out of their homes by their parents because of their homosexual identity or behavior (NASW, 1993).

6. The sociology of family literature refers to new families formed through remarriage as "binuclear" and "refamilies" (Ahrons and Rodgers, 1994.) Note these "postmodern" descriptions of families of runaways from my sample:

> I have lots of other brothers and sisters, but she's the only one who lives with us. I have a lot of half brothers and sisters—my mom's got me, my sister Melinda, who is thirteen years old, my brother Jeremy, who is ten years old, my other sister is five years old, then I have a half sister and brothers: Lorena, who is seven years old, and Mark, who is only two years old. Well, Melinda, Jeremy, Lorena, and Mark all live with their dads—they have two dads, with two kids each. I have my dad Jesse, my little sister Lois has her dad Lee, and my sister and brother, Lorena and Jeremy, have their dad. My Mom is the mom of everybody, except for Lorena and Mark. (Amy)

> After my Mom and Dad got divorced, my Dad got remarried. So now I have one real sister, a stepsister, a half sister, and my little brother—my real little brother. He has the same dad as me and the same mom. The half sister has the same mom, and the stepsister is Jennifer's daughter, my dad's new wife. (Jesse)

7. See, for example, Judith Stacey's study, *Brave New Families* (1991).

8. Of this study's participants, 77 percent reported experiencing physical abuse, 35 percent sexual abuse, and 31 percent both. One participant was abandoned by his mother at age fourteen.

9. A full discussion of anger and running away from physical abuse is presented in Chapter 4: "The Politics of Anger: Rebellion, *Ressentiment*, and Emotional Capital."

10. Statutory rape is a criminal offense, varying by state, occurring when sexual activity takes place between a minor under the age of sixteen and an adult over eighteen years old, or when there is four or more years difference between the adult and the minor.

11. Nineteen percent of the participants actually raised similar issues of violations of diaries and privacy.

12. She is speaking of her custodial guardian, an aunt, not a parent.

13. Whether it is even advisable to attempt rapprochement in child abuse situations is also questionable (Bass and Davis, 1988, p. 149). Also, an excellent and compelling detailed discussion of the meaning and implications of moral hatred and forgiveness can be found in Murphy and Hampton (1988).

14. Before we jump to label Carmen "promiscuous" or "delinquent," remember that "drug abuse, alcohol abuse, tobacco addiction, gunslaughter, drunk driv-

ing, out-of-wedlock births, illiteracy, racism, and sexism were adult problems before we taught them or allowed teenagers to experience them" (Brennan, Huizinga, and Elliott, 1978, p. 65). One scholar notes that teenagers are learning their sins from adults:

> The use and abuse of drugs, alcohol, and tobacco were all adult problems first and became teenage problems only after we introduced youngsters to them as indicators of an adult lifestyle. Other adult-proclaimed youth problems such as unemployment and delinquent behavior follow the same demographic and cyclical patterns among youth as they do among adults. (Ianni, 1989, p. 50)

As one clever runaway noted:

> It's like my mom thinks I'm doing all these things like drugs and stuff. I am not; I have never done any drugs in my life—I don't even smoke! And she thinks that I'm doin' all this stuff. . . . Now my boyfriend, he smokes pot and drinks and stuff . . . but my mom does that stuff too! (Princess)

15. See also Ogbu (1978), Fordham (1993), Fordham and Ogbu (1986), and Fine (1991).

16. Independent living programs are model programs that were developed in the late 1980s in various regions in the United States. They respond to the need to give certain eligible older youths the opportunity to get out of the foster family/runaway cycle and begin to live on their own in apartments and work. This kind of arrangement is meant to serve as a safe transition to independent adult living. Publicly funded and administered on the local level, not many of these slots are available, and there is much controversy surrounding the policy. Basically, a social service office oversees an apartment building and fills it with teens who are trying to live on their own. The social workers help place them in jobs, help them learn how to shop and cook, and teach them how to budget, balance a checkbook, and pay the rent. Problems do arise—such as drug use in the buildings and missed rent payments—that are complicated to resolve and carry complex ramifications.

17. Given that teenage runaways are facing profound dilemmas such as incest and suicide, it is understandable that often-incomprehensible algebra must pale in importance by comparison.

18. I call it the "I can put my mother down, but you can't" syndrome.

19. Bass and Davis discuss the misplaced loyalty and denial that some abuse victims develop as a coping mechanism in order to survive, which may be the case with Roy (1988, p. 42).

20. He's naming various shelter staff members.

21. At this shelter, if the youths are criminal offenders then they occupy Department of Youth Services slots rather than Department of Social Services allotments: this designates their placements in the shelter, and in the juvenile system, as juvenile offenders.

22. Later she admitted that her boyfriend was twenty-seven years old. (Jean was fifteen years old.)

23. This was the notation in Eric's file.

24. Running away from home due to overly arbitrary parents who are too strict in enforcing house rules was cited as the primary reason by 11 percent of the participants in this study, 19 percent cited being arrested as the main reason that they were in the shelter, and 19 percent cited family conflict as the primary reason for running away (these two—arrested and conflict—I grouped together under a heading of general family conflict—forming 38 percent of the sample); 46 percent of the youths in my sample cited that they were running away from physical and sexual abuse, and 4 percent were abandoned.

25. When runaways reported that they felt rejected and perceived themselves as unimportant to the family, their motivation to meet family norms seemed to weaken.

Chapter 4

1. For African-American children, that figure jumps to 37.2 percent; among Hispanic [sic] teenagers, 34.4 percent live in poverty (U.S. Bureau of Census, 1992, p. 48).

2. We don't know if that was necessarily a positive event for her mother to have dated an older man. It is possible that her mother was attempting to give her daughter some well-earned cautionary advice. However, we do know that such interactions produced resentment and anger in the youths, and they reported that it made them want to run away.

3. I use the term "power" more metaphorically than in the strict Weberian sense, for example, a boss has power over a worker, a man has power over a woman, a parent has power over a child.

Chapter 5

1. Kate gives her DSS worker a positive review, but she's still "working the system" so she can use her visits to the counselor as a chance to have a clandestine meeting with her boyfriend!

Bibliography

Adams, Gerald, Thomas Gullotta, and Mary Anne Clancy. 1985. "Homeless Adolescents: A Descriptive Study of Similarities Between Runaways and Throwaways." *Adolescence*, xx(79), Fall, pp. 715-724.

Adams, Gerald and Gordon Munro. 1979. "Portrait of the North American Runaway: A Critical Review." *Journal of Youth and Adolescence*, 8(3), pp. 359-373.

Adler, Jerry. 1994. "Kids Growing Up Scared: Our Kids Are Robbed of Their Childhoods," *Newsweek*, January 10, pp. 43-50.

Ahrons, Constance and Roy H. Rodgers. 1994. "The Remarriage Transition." In Arlene Skolnick and Jerome Skolnick, Eds., *Family in Transition*, Eighth Edition. New York: HarperCollins, pp. 257-272.

American Psychiatric Association. 1968. *Diagnostic and Statistical Manual of Mental Disorders*, Second Edition. Washington, DC: American Psychiatric Association.

Appathurai, Carol. 1991. "Developing Policies for Runaways: Insights from the Literature. *Journal of Health and Social Policy*, 2(4), pp. 51-64.

Aries, Philippe. 1962. *Centuries of Childhood*. New York: Vintage.

Axthelm, Pete. 1988. "Somebody Else's Kids." *Newsweek*, April 25, pp. 64-68.

Bass, Deborah. 1992. *Helping Vulnerable Youths: Runaway and Homeless Adolescents in the United States*. Washington, DC: National Association of Social Workers.

Bass, Ellen and Laura Davis. 1988. *The Courage to Heal: A Guide for Women Survivors of Child Sexual Abuse*. New York: Perennial Library.

Becker, Howard. 1963. *Outsiders*. Glencoe, IL: The Free Press.

Bedford, Errol. 1984. "Emotions." In Cheshire Calhoun and Robert Solomon, Eds., *What Is An Emotion?* New York: Oxford University Press, pp. 264-278.

Berg, Bruce. 1989. "A Dramaturgical Look at Interviewing." *Qualitative Research Methods for the Social Sciences*. Boston, MA: Allyn and Bacon.

Blau, Melinda. 1979. "Why Parents Kick Their Kids Out." *Parents*, April, pp. 65-69.

Blumer, Herbert. 1969. *Symbolic Interactionism: Perspective and Method*. Englewood Cliffs, NJ: Prentice Hall.

Bourdieu, Pierre. 1977. "Cultural Reproduction and Social Reproduction." In Jerome Karabel and Albert H. Halsey, Eds., *Power and Ideology*. New York: Oxford University Press, pp. 487-511.

Brazil, Eric. 1993. "No More Shelter: 200 Huddle in Terminal Tagged for Closure at Night." *San Francisco Examiner*, February 12, pp. A1, A21.

Brennan, Tim. 1980. "Mapping the Diversity Among Runaways: A Descriptive Multivariate Analysis of Selected Social Psychological Background Conditions." *Journal of Family Issues*, 1(2), June, pp. 189-209.

Brennan, Tim, David Huizinga, and Delbert Elliott. 1978. *The Social Psychology of Runaways*. Lexington, MA: Lexington Books.

Brown, Marjorie. 1979. "Teenage Prostitution." *Adolescence*, 14(56), pp. 665-680.

Bumpass, Larry. 1990. "What's Happening to the Family? Interactions Between Demographic and Institutional Change." *Demography*, 27(4), November, pp. 483-498.

Burgess, Anne. 1986. *Youth at Risk: Understanding Runaway and Exploited Youth*. Washington, DC: National Center for Missing and Exploited Children.

Butler, Pamela. 1991. *Talking to Yourself*. San Francisco, CA: Harper.

Calhoun, Chesire and Robert C. Solomon, Eds. 1984. *What Is an Emotion? Classical Readings in Philosophical Psychology*. New York: Oxford University Press.

Cheal, David. 1991. *Family and the State of Theory*. Toronto, Canada: University of Toronto Press.

Chodorow, Nancy. 1989. "Family Structure and Feminine Personality." In Laurel Richardson and Verta Taylor, Eds., *Feminist Frontiers II: Rethinking Sex, Gender, and Society*. New York: McGraw-Hill, pp. 43-57.

Collins, Don and Peter Gabor. 1988. "Helping Children with Cathartic Disclosure of Trauma." *Journal of Child Care*, 3(6), pp. 25-38.

Collins, Patricia Hill. 1991. *Black Feminist Thought: Knowledge, Consciousness, and the Politics of Empowerment*. New York: Routledge.

Davitz, Joel. 1969. *The Language of Emotion*. New York: London Press.

Demo, David. 1994. "Parent-Child Relations: Assessing Recent Changes." In Arlene Skolnick and Jerome Skolnick, Eds., *Family in Transition*, Eighth Edition. New York: HarperCollins, pp. 294-313.

Denzin, Norman K. 1984. *On Understanding Emotion*. San Francisco, CA: Jossey-Bass Publishers.

Desetta, Al, Ed. 1994. *Foster Care Youth United*. New York: Youth Communications.

DeVault, Marjorie. 1990. "Talking and Listening from Women's Standpoint: Feminist Strategies for Interviewing and Analysis." *Social Problems*, 37(1), February, pp. 96-117.

Dornbusch, Sanford M. 1991. *The Stanford Studies of Homeless Families, Children, and Youth*. Stanford, CA: Stanford University, The Stanford Center for the Study of Families, Children, and Youth.

Durkheim, Émile. 1961. *Moral Education*. Glencoe, IL: The Free Press.

Dusek, Jerome B. 1991. *Adolescent Development and Behavior*, Second Edition. Englewood Cliffs, NJ: Prentice Hall.

Ek, Carl and Lala Steelman. 1988. "Becoming a Runaway: From the Accounts of Youthful Runners." *Youth and Society*, 19(3), March, pp. 334-358.

Erikson, Eric. 1950. *Childhood and Society*. New York: Norton.

Feldman, Shirley S. and Glen R. Elliott. 1990. *At the Threshold: The Developing Adolescent*. Cambridge, MA: Harvard University Press.

Feldman, Shirley S. and Thomas M. Gehring. 1990. "Changing Perceptions of Family Cohesion and Power Across Adolescence." In Rolf E. Muus, Ed., *Adolescent Behavior and Society*. New York: McGraw-Hill, pp. 145-156.

Fernandez, Manny. 1998. "Nobody's Child: Three Part Series of Haight Street Runaways." *San Francisco Chronicle*, November 17, 18, 19, p. A1 each day.

Fine, Michelle. 1991. *Framing Dropouts: Notes on the Politics of an Urban Public High School.* Albany, NY: State University Press.

Finkelhor, David, Gerald Hotaling, and Andrea Sedlak. 1990. "Missing, Abducted, Runaway, and Thrownaway Children in America—First Report: Numbers and Characteristics, National Incidence Studies." Washington, DC: U.S. Department of Justice, Office of Justice Programs, Office of Juvenile Justice and Delinquency Prevention.

Fordham, Signithia. 1993. "Those Loud Black Girls: (Black) Women, Silence, and Gender 'Passing' in the Academy." *Anthropology and Education Quarterly,* 24(1), pp. 3-32.

Fordham, Signithia and John Ogbu. 1986. "Black Students' Success: Coping with the Burden of 'Acting White,' " *The Urban Review,* 18(3), pp. 176-206.

Furstenberg Jr., Frank F. and Andrew J. Cherlin. 1994. "Children's Adjustment to Divorce." In Arlene Skolnick and Jerome Skolnick, Eds., *Family in Transition,* Eighth Edition. New York: HarperCollins, pp. 314-324.

Garbarino, James, Cynthia J. Schellenbach, and Janet M. Sebes. 1986. *Troubled Youths, Troubled Families: Understanding Families At Risk for Adolescent Maltreatment.* New York: Aldine Publishing.

Gilligan, Carol, Annie Rogers, and Deborah Tolman, Eds. 1991. *Women, Girls, and Psychotherapy: Reframing Resistance.* Binghamton, NY: The Haworth Press, Inc.

Glaser, Barry G. and Anselm L. Strauss. 1967. *The Discovery of Grounded Theory.* Chicago, IL: Aldine.

Glazer, Myron. 1972. *The Research Adventure: Problems and Promise of Field Work.* New York: Random House.

Glazer, Myron. 1982. "The Threat of the Stranger: Vulnerability, Reciprocity, and Fieldwork." In Joan E. Sieber, Ed., *The Ethics of Social Research.* New York: Springer Verlag, pp. 49-70.

Glick, Paul C. 1994. "American Families: As They Are and Were." In Arlene Skolnick and Jerome Skolnick, Eds., *Family in Transition,* Eighth Edition. New York: HarperCollins, pp. 91-103.

Goffman, Erving. 1963. *Stigma: Notes on the Management of Spoiled Identity.* New York: Simon and Schuster.

Gorov, Lynda. 1994. "Our Wounded Youth." *Boston Sunday Globe,* March 6, pp. A1, A14.

Hammersley, Martyn and Paul Atkinson. 1983. *Ethnography: Principles in Practice.* New York: Routledge.

Harré, Rom, Ed. 1986. *The Social Construction of Emotions.* New York: Basil Blackwell, Inc.

Hartman, Carol, Ann W. Burgess, and Arlene McCormack. 1987. "Pathways and Cycles of Runaways: A Model for Understanding Repetitive Runaway Behavior." *Hospital and Community Psychiatry,* March, pp. 292-299.

Herbert, Bob. 1994. "Deadly Data on Handguns." *The New York Times*, March 3, p. A15.

Hersch, Patricia. 1988. "Coming of Age on City Streets." *Psychology Today*, 22(1), January, pp. 29-37.

Hirschi, Travis. 1985 [1969]. "A Control Theory of Delinquency." In Stuart Traub and Craig Little, Eds., *Theories of Deviance*. Itasca, IL: F. E. Peacock Publishers, Inc., pp. 257-273.

Hirshberg, David L., Eric Masi, Elaine Harrington, Robert Kelley, Deirdre Maltais Heisler, and John Shaw. 1988. "Summary of the Workshop: Why They Run from Treatment and What We Can Do." *Journal of Child Care*, Special Issue, pp. 49-57.

Hochschild, Arlie Russell. 1975. "The Sociology of Feeling and Emotion." In Marcia Millman and Rosabeth Moss Kanter, Eds., *Another Voice*. Garden City, NY: Anchor Press/Doubleday.

Hochschild, Arlie Russell. 1983. *The Managed Heart: Commercialization of Human Feeling*. Berkeley, CA: University of California Press.

Holdaway, Doris M. and JoAnn Ray. 1992. "Attitudes of Street Kids Toward Foster Care." *Child and Adolescent Social Work Journal*, 9(4), August, pp. 307-317.

Ianni, Francis A. J. 1989. *The Search for Structure: A Report on American Youth Today*. New York: Free Press.

Jankowski, Martin Sanchez. 1991. *Islands in the Street: Gangs and American Society*. Berkeley, CA: University of California Press.

Janus, Mark-David, Arlene McCormack, Ann W. Burgess, and Carol Hartman. 1987. *Adolescent Runaways: Causes and Consequences*. Lexington, MA: Lexington Books.

Jenkins, R. L. 1971. "The Runaway Reaction." *American Journal of Psychiatry*, 128(2), pp. 1032-1039.

Jones, Loring. 1988. "A Typology of Adolescent Runaways." *Child and Adolescent Social Work Journal*, 5(1), Spring, pp. 16-29.

Katz, Jack. 1988. *Seductions of Crime: Moral and Sensual Attractions in Doing Evil*. New York: Basic Books.

Kemper, Theodore D. 1978. *A Social Interactional Theory of Emotions*. New York: Wiley.

Kemper, Theodore D. 1981. "Social Constructionist and Positivist Approaches to the Sociology of Emotions." *American Journal of Sociology*, 87(2), pp. 336-362.

Kennedy, Michael. 1991. "Homeless and Runaway Youth Mental Health Issues: No Access to the System." *Journal of Adolescent Health*, 12, pp. 576-579.

Kett, Joseph, 1997. *Rites of Passage: Adolescence in America, 1790 to the Present*. New York: Basic Books.

Kruks, Gabe. 1991. "Gay and Lesbian Homeless/Street Youth: Special Issues and Concerns." *Journal of Adolescent Health*, 12(7), pp. 515-518.

Kufeldt, Kathleen and Philip Perry. 1989. "Running Around with Runaways." *Community Alternatives*, 1(1), Spring, pp. 85-97.

Kurtz, David P., Gail L. Kurtz, and Sara V. Jarvis. 1991. "Problems of Maltreated Runaway Youth." *Adolescence*, 26(103), Fall, pp. 543-555.

Kutner, Lawrence. 1994. "How to Handle News That Teen Wants to Move Out of Your Home." *Springfield Union News*, April 12.

Leadbeater, Bonnie Ross and Niobe Way, Eds. 1996. *Urban Girls: Resisting Stereotypes, Creating Identities*. New York: New York University Press.

Levine, Robert A. and Merry White. 1994. "The Social Transformation of Childhood." In Arlene Skolnick and Jerome Skolnick, Eds., *Family in Transition*, Eighth Edition. New York: HarperCollins, pp. 273-293.

Libertoff, Ken. 1980. "The Runaway Child in America: A Social History." *Journal of Family Issues*, 1(2), June, pp. 151-164.

Lofland, John and Lyn H. Lofland. 1984. *Analyzing Social Settings: A Guide to Qualitative Observation and Analysis*, Second Edition. Belmont, CA: Wadsworth Publishing Company.

Luker, Kristin. 1991. "Dubious Conceptions: The Controversy Over Teen Pregnancy." *The American Prospect*, (5), Spring, pp. 73-83.

MacLeod, Jay. 1987. *Ain't No Makin' It: Leveled Aspirations in a Low-Income Neighborhood*. Boulder, CO: Westview Press.

McCarthy, Bill and John Hagan. 1992. "Surviving on the Street: The Experiences of Homeless Youth." *Journal of Adolescent Research*, 7(4), October, pp. 412-430.

McEvoy, Charles and Edsel L. Erickson. 1990. *Youth and Exploitation*. Montreal: Learning Publications, Inc.

Merton, Robert. 1968. *Social Theory and Social Structure*. New York: The Free Press.

Merton, Robert. 1985. "Social Structure and Anomie." In Stuart Traub and Craig Little, Eds., *Theories of Deviance*. Itasca, IL: F. E. Peacock Publishers, Inc., pp. 107-131.

Merton, Robert and P. L. Kendall 1946. "The Focused Interview." *American Journal of Sociology*, 51, pp. 541-557.

Mesa-Bains, Amalia and Owen Barajas Dallas. 1986. *At Risk: Demystifying the Dropout—Awareness, Intervention, Enlistment*. San Francisco, CA: San Francisco Unified School District.

Miller, Dorothy, et al. 1980. *Runaways: Illegal Aliens in Their Own Land*. New York: J. F. Bergin Publishers.

Miller, Patricia Y. 1979. "Female Delinquency: Fact and Fiction." In Max Sugar, Ed., *Female Adolescent Development*. New York: Brunner/Mazel, pp. 115-140.

Mintz, Steven and Susan Kellogg. 1988. *Domestic Revolutions: A Social History of American Family Life*. New York: Free Press.

Modell, John. 1989. *Into One's Own: From Youth to Adulthood in the United States, 1920-1975*. Berkeley, CA: University of California Press.

Modell, John and Madeline Goodman. 1990. "Historical Perspectives." In S. Shirley Feldman and Glen R. Elliott, Eds., *At The Threshold: The Developing Adolescent*. Cambridge, MA: Harvard University Press, pp. 93-123.

Montemayor, Raymond. 1990. "Parents and Adolescents in Conflict." In Rolf E. Muss, Ed., *Adolescent Behavior and Society*. New York: McGraw-Hill, pp. 130-144.

Murphy, Jeffrie G. and Jean Hampton. 1988. *Forgiveness and Mercy.* New York: Cambridge University Press.

Myers, David G. 1990. *Exploring Psychology.* New York: Worth Publishers, Inc.

Nannis, Ellen D. and Philip A. Cowan. 1987. "Emotional Understanding: A Matter of Age, Dimension, and Point of View." *Journal of Applied Developmental Psychology*, 8, pp. 289-304.

National Association of Social Workers (NASW). 1993. *Executive Summary: 1992 Update to a National Survey of Programs for Runaway and Homeless Youths and a Model Service Delivery Approach.* Washington DC: U.S. Department of Health and Human Services.

National Network of Runaway and Youth Services. 1991. *To Whom Do They Belong? Runaway, Homeless, and Other Youth in High-Risk Situations in the 1990s.* Washington, DC: The National Network.

National Network of Runaway and Youth Services. 1994. *Runaway and Homeless Youth Fact Sheet.* Washington, DC: The National Network, February.

National Runaway Switchboard. 1993. *Why Children Run Away: Fact Sheet.* Chicago, IL: National Runaway Switchboard.

"New Survey of Runway Youths." *San Francisco Chronicle,* January 2, 1992, p. A3.

Nye, F. Ivan. 1980. "A Theoretical Perspective on Running Away." *Journal of Family Issues*, Volume 1, Number 2, June, pp. 274-299.

Nye, F. Ivan. 1985 [1958]. "Family Relationships and Delinquent Behavior." In Stuart Traub and Craig Little, Eds., *Theories of Deviance.* Itasca, IL: F. E. Peacock Publishers Inc., pp. 243-251.

Ogbu, John. 1978. *Minority Education and Caste: The American System in Cross-Cultural Perspective.* New York: Academic Press.

O'Neill, John. 1994. *The Missing Child in Liberal Theory: Towards a Covenant Theory of Family, Community, Welfare, and the Civic State.* Toronto, Canada: University of Toronto.

Palenski, Joseph. 1984. *Kids Who Run Away.* Saratoga, CA: R & E Publishers.

Palenski, Joseph and Harold Launer. 1987. "The Process of Running Away: A Redefinition." *Adolescence*, 22(86), Summer, pp. 347-362.

Parsons, Talcott and Robert Bales. 1960. *The Family, Socialization and Interaction Process.* Glencoe, IL: Free Press.

Piaget, Jean. 1932. *The Moral Judgement of the Child.* New York: Harcourt, Brace and World.

Pipher, Mary. 1994. *Reviving Ophelia: Saving the Lives of Adolescent Girls.* New York: Ballantine Books.

Pogrebin, Letty Cottin. 1983. *Family Politics.* New York: McGraw-Hill.

Popenoe, David. 1988. *Disturbing the Nest: Family Change and Decline in Modern Societies.* New York: Aldine de Gruyter.

Powers, Jane Levine and Barbara Weiss Jaklitsch. 1989. *Understanding Survivors of Abuse: Stories of Homeless and Runaway Adolescents.* Lexinton, MA: Lexington Books.

Rader, Datson. 1985. "I Want to Die So I Won't Hurt No More." *Parade Magazine*, August 18, pp. 4-6.

Reiss, Albert J. 1951. "Delinquency As a Failure of Personal and Social Controls." *American Sociological Review,* 16, April, pp. 196-207.

Roberts, Albert R. 1982. "Adolescent Runways in Suburbia: A New Typology." *Adolescence,* 17(66), Summer, pp. 387-396.

Robertson, Ian. 1987. *Sociology,* Third Edition. New York: Worth Publishers.

Robertson, Marjorie and Milton Greenblatt. 1992. *Homelessness: A National Perspective.* New York: Plenum Press.

Rollins, Judith. 1985. *Between Women: Domestics and Their Employers.* Philadelphia, PA: Temple University Press.

Rothman, Jack. 1991. *Runaways and Homeless Youth: Strengthening Services to Families and Children.* New York: Longman.

Rubin, Lillian. 1976. *Worlds of Pain: Life in the Working-Class Family.* New York: Basic Books.

Rubin, Lillian. 1994. "The Culture of Adolescent Sexuality." In Arlene Skolnick and Jerome Skolnick, Eds., *Family in Transition,* Eighth Edition. New York: HarperCollins, pp. 157-164.

San Franciscans Against Proposition J. 1992. *Facts on Homelessness and Poverty in San Francisco.* San Francisco, CA.

Scheff, Thomas J. 1990. *Microsociology: Discourse, Emotion, and Social Structure.* Chicago, IL: University of Chicago Press.

Scheler, Max. 1961. *Ressentiment.* William Holdheim, Trans., Glencoe, IL: Free Press.

Sharlin, Shlomo. 1992. "Runaway Girls in Distress: Motivation, Background, and Personality." *Adolescence,* 27(106), Summer, pp. 387-405.

Shott, Susan. 1979. "Emotion and Social Life: A Symbolic Interactionist Analysis." *American Journal of Sociology,* 84(6), pp. 1317-1334.

Skiba, Katherine. 1989. "On the Run and Searching for Answers." *The Milwaukee Journal,* Thursday, January 12, p. 1.

Skolnick, Arlene and Jerome Skolnick, Eds. 1994. *Family in Transition,* Eighth Edition. New York: HarperCollins

Spelman, Elizabeth. 1989. "Anger and Insubordination." In Ann Garry and Marilyn Pearsall, Eds., *Women, Knowledge, and Reality: Explorations in Feminist Philosophy.* Boston, MA: Unwin Hyman, pp. 263-273.

Stacey, Judith. 1991. *Brave New Families.* New York: Basic Books.

Steinberg, Laurence. 1990. "Autonomy, Conflict, and Harmony in the Family Relationship." In S. Shirley Feldman and Glenn R. Elliott, Eds., *At the Threshold.* Cambridge, MA: Harvard University Press, pp. 255-276.

Steiner, Claude. 1986. *When a Man Loves a Woman: Sexual and Emotional Literacy for the Modern Man.* New York: Grove Press.

Stiffman, Arlene. "Physical and Sexual Abuse in Runaway Youths." *Child Abuse and Neglect,* 13, pp. 417-426.

Strauss, Anselm and Juliet Corbin. 1990. *Basics of Qualitative Research: Grounded Theory Procedures and Techniques.* London: Sage.

Sutherland, Edwin and Donald Cressey. 1985 (1978). "The Theory of Differential Association." In Delos Kelly, Ed., *Deviant Behavior.* New York: St. Martin's Press, pp. 125-131.

Sykes, Gresham and David Matza. 1985 [1957]. "Techniques of Neutralization: A Theory of Delinquency." In Stuart Traub and Craig Little, Eds., *Theories of Deviance.* Itasca, IL: F. E. Peacock Publishers, pp. 207-215.

Thomas, William Isaac. 1963. *The Unadjusted Girl.* New York: Harper and Row.

Thompson, Sharon. 1995. *Going All the Way: Teenage Girls' Tales of Sex, Romance, and Pregnancy.* New York: Hill and Wang.

Towers, Kay. 1985. Female Adolescent Runaways and Intergenerational Patterns of Separation: A Familial Perspective. Unpublished dissertation, Smith College School for Social Work, Northhampton, MA.

Traub, Stuart and Craig Little, Eds. 1985. *Theories of Deviance.* Itasca, IL: F. E. Peacock Publishers.

Uhlenberg, Peter and David Eggebeen. 1986. "The Declining Well-Being of American Adolescents." *Public Interest,* 82, Winter, pp. 25-38.

U.S. Bureau of the Census. 1992. *Current Population Reports, P23-181. Households, Families and Children: A 30-Year Perspective.* Washington, DC: U.S. Government Printing Office.

U.S. Department of Health and Human Services. 1995. "Youth with Runaway, Throwaway, and Homeless Experience: Prevalence, Drug Use, and Other At-Risk Behaviors." *Volume 1: Final Report.* Washington, DC: Administration on Children, Youth, and Families.

U.S. Department of Justice. 1989. "Runaway Children and the Juvenile Justice and Delinquency Prevention Act: What Is the Impact?" *Juvenile Justice Bulletin.* Washington, DC: Office of Juvenile Justice and Delinquency Prevention; National Institute for Juvenile Justice and Delinquency Prevention, May.

U.S. Department of Justice. 1990. *Juvenile Court Statistics 1990.* Washington, DC: Office of Justice Programs, Office of Juvenile Justice and Delinquency Prevention.

U.S. Department of Justice Fact Sheet. 1990. "Fact Sheet on Missing Children." Washington, DC: Office of Juvenile Justice and Delinquency Prevention.

U.S. General Accounting Office (USGAO). 1989. *Homelessness: Homeless and Runaway Youth Receiving Services at Federally Funded Shelters.* Washington, DC: United States General Accounting Office, December.

Van Maanen, John. 1988. *Tales of the Field: On Writing Ethnography.* Chicago, IL: University of Chicago Press.

Waring, Nancy. 1993. "Who's Delinquent?" *The Boston Globe Magazine,* October 17, pp. 14-34.

Wells, Mona and Harjit Sandhu. 1986. "The Juvenile Runaway: A Historical Perspective." *Free Inquiry in Creative Sociology,* 14(2), November, pp. 143-147.

Wilkinson, Annette. 1987. "Born to Rebel: An Ethnography of Street Kids." In *Dissertation Abstracts International,* 48, 12(1), June, pp. 1-20.

Yates, Gary, Richard MacKenzie, Julia Pennbridge, and Avon Swofford. 1991. "A Risk Profile Comparison of Homeless Youth Involved in Prostitution and Homeless Youth Not Involved." *Journal of Adolescent Health*, 12(7), 545-548.

Zide, Marylyn R. 1990. Social Bonds: Running To, Running From, Thrown Out, and Forsaken Youth. Unpublished dissertation. Miami, FL: Barry University, Ellen Whiteside McDonnell School of Social Work.

Index

Page numbers followed by the letter "n" indicate notes.

HAWORTH Social Work Practice
Carlton E. Munson, DSW, Senior Editor

SOCIAL WORK PRACTICE IN THE MILITARY by James G. Daley. (1999).

GROUP WORK: SKILLS AND STRATEGIES FOR EFFECTIVE INTERVEN-TIONS, SECOND EDITION by Sondra Brandler and Camille P. Roman. (1999). "A clear, basic description of what group work requires, including what skills and techniques group workers need to be effective." *Hospital and Community Psychiatry* (from the first edition)

TEENAGE RUNAWAYS: BROKEN HEARTS AND "BAD ATTITUDES" by Laurie Schaffner. (1999). "Great insight and sensitivity. Schaffner's groundbreaking work challenges traditional criminology that relies mainly on individualistic and male-centered approaches." *Esther Madriz, PhD, Assistant Professor, Sociology Department, University of San Francisco*

CELEBRATING DIVERSITY: COEXISTING IN A MULTICULTURAL SOCIETY by Benyamin Chetkow-Yanoov. (1999). "Makes a valuable contribution to peace theory and practice." *Ian Harris, EdD, Executive Secretary, Peace Education Committee, International Peace Research Association*

SOCIAL WELFARE POLICY ANALYSIS AND CHOICES by Hobart A. Burch. (1999). "Will become the landmark text in its field for many decades to come." *Sheldon Rahn, DSW, Founding Dean and Emeritus Professor of Social Policy and Social Administration, Faculty of Social Work, Wilfrid Laurier University, Canada*

SOCIAL WORK PRACTICE: A SYSTEMS APPROACH, SECOND EDITION by Benyamin Chetkow-Yanoov. (1999)."Highly recommended as a primary text for any and all introductory social work courses." *Ram A. Cnaan, PhD, Associate Professor, School of Social Work, University of Pennsylvania*

CRITICAL SOCIAL WELFARE ISSUES: TOOLS FOR SOCIAL WORK AND HEALTH CARE PROFESSIONALS edited by Arthur J. Katz, Abraham Lurie, and Carlos M. Vidal. (1997). "Offers hopeful agendas for change, while navigating the societal challenges facing those in the human services today." *Book News Inc.*

SOCIAL WORK IN HEALTH SETTINGS: PRACTICE IN CONTEXT, SECOND EDITION edited by Toba Schwaber Kerson. (1997). "A first-class document. . . . It will be found among the steadier and lasting works on the social work aspects of American health care." *Hans S. Falck, PhD, Professor Emeritus and Former Chair, Health Specialization in Social Work, Virginia Commonwealth University*

PRINCIPLES OF SOCIAL WORK PRACTICE: A GENERIC PRACTICE APPROACH by Molly R. Hancock. (1997). "Hancock's discussions advocate reflection and self-awareness to create a climate for client change." *Journal of Social Work Education*

NOBODY'S CHILDREN: ORPHANS OF THE HIV EPIDEMIC by Steven F. Dansky. (1997). "Professionally sound, moving, and useful for both professionals and interested readers alike." *Ellen G. Friedman, ACSW, Associate Director of Support Services, Beth Israel Medical Center, Methadone Maintenance Treatment Program*

SOCIAL WORK APPROACHES TO CONFLICT RESOLUTION: MAKING FIGHTING OBSOLETE by Benyamin Chetkow-Yanoov. (1996). "Presents an examination of the nature and cause of conflict and suggests techniques for coping with conflict." *Journal of Criminal Justice*

FEMINIST THEORIES AND SOCIAL WORK: APPROACHES AND APPLICATIONS by Christine Flynn Saulnier. (1996). "An essential reference to be read repeatedly by all educators and practitioners who are eager to learn more about feminist theory and practice." *Nancy R. Hooyman, PhD, Dean and Professor, School of Social Work, University of Washington, Seattle*

THE RELATIONAL SYSTEMS MODEL FOR FAMILY THERAPY: LIVING IN THE FOUR REALITIES by Donald R. Bardill. (1996). "Engages the reader in quiet, thoughtful conversation on the timeless issue of helping families and individuals." *Christian Counseling Resource Review*

SOCIAL WORK INTERVENTION IN AN ECONOMIC CRISIS: THE RIVER COMMUNITIES PROJECT by Martha Baum and Pamela Twiss. (1996). "Sets a standard for universities in terms of the types of meaningful roles they can play in supporting and sustaining communities." *Kenneth J. Jaros, PhD, Director, Public Health Social Work Training Program, University of Pittsburgh*

FUNDAMENTALS OF COGNITIVE-BEHAVIOR THERAPY: FROM BOTH SIDES OF THE DESK by Bill Borcherdt. (1996). "Both beginning and experienced practitioners . . . will find a considerable number of valuable suggestions in Borcherdt's book." *Albert Ellis, PhD, President, Institute for Rational-Emotive Therapy, New York City*

BASIC SOCIAL POLICY AND PLANNING: STRATEGIES AND PRACTICE METHODS by Hobart A. Burch. (1996). "Burch's familiarity with his topic is evident and his book is an easy introduction to the field." *Readings*

THE CROSS-CULTURAL PRACTICE OF CLINICAL CASE MANAGEMENT IN MENTAL HEALTH edited by Peter Manoleas. (1996). "Makes a contribution by bringing together the cross-cultural and clinical case management perspectives in working with those who have serious mental illness." *Disability Studies Quarterly*

FAMILY BEYOND FAMILY: THE SURROGATE PARENT IN SCHOOLS AND OTHER COMMUNITY AGENCIES by Sanford Weinstein. (1995). "Highly recommended to anyone concerned about the welfare of our children and the breakdown of the American family." *Jerrold S. Greenberg, EdD, Director of Community Service, College of Health & Human Performance, University of Maryland*

PEOPLE WITH HIV AND THOSE WHO HELP THEM: CHALLENGES, INTEGRATION, INTERVENTION by R. Dennis Shelby. (1995). "A useful and compassionate contribution to the HIV psychotherapy literature." *Public Health*

THE BLACK ELDERLY: SATISFACTION AND QUALITY OF LATER LIFE by Marguerite Coke and James A. Twaite. (1995). "Presents a model for predicting life satisfaction in this population." *Abstracts in Social Gerontology*

BUILDING ON WOMEN'S STRENGTHS: A SOCIAL WORK AGENDA FOR THE TWENTY-FIRST CENTURY edited by Liane V. Davis. (1994). "The most lucid and accessible overview of the related epistemological debates in the social work literature." *Journal of the National Association of Social Workers*

NOW DARE EVERYTHING: TALES OF HIV-RELATED PSYCHOTHERAPY by Steven F. Dansky. (1994). "A highly recommended book for anyone working with persons who are HIV positive. . . . Every library should have a copy of this book." *AIDS Book Review Journal*

INTERVENTION RESEARCH: DESIGN AND DEVELOPMENT FOR HUMAN SERVICE edited by Jack Rothman and Edwin J. Thomas. (1994). "Provides a useful framework for the further examination of methodology for each separate step of such research." *Academic Library Book Review*

FORENSIC SOCIAL WORK: LEGAL ASPECTS OF PROFESSIONAL PRACTICE by Robert L. Barker and Douglas M. Branson. (1993). "The authors combine their expertise to create this informative guide to address legal practice issues facing social workers." *Newsletter of the National Organization of Forensic Social Work*

CLINICAL SOCIAL WORK SUPERVISION, SECOND EDITION by Carlton E. Munson. (1993). "A useful, thorough, and articulate reference for supervisors and for 'supervisees' who are wanting to understand their supervisor or are looking for effective supervision." *Transactional Analysis Journal*

ELEMENTS OF THE HELPING PROCESS: A GUIDE FOR CLINICIANS by Raymond Fox. (1993). "Filled with helpful hints, creative interventions, and practical guidelines." *Journal of Family Psychotherapy*

IF A PARTNER HAS AIDS: GUIDE TO CLINICAL INTERVENTION FOR RELATIONSHIPS IN CRISIS by R. Dennis Shelby. (1993). "A welcome addition to existing publications about couples coping with AIDS, it offers intervention ideas and strategies to clinicians." *Contemporary Psychology*

GERONTOLOGICAL SOCIAL WORK SUPERVISION by Ann Burack-Weiss and Frances Coyle Brennan. (1991). "The creative ideas in this book will aid supervisors working with students and experienced social workers." *Senior News*

SOCIAL WORK THEORY AND PRACTICE WITH THE TERMINALLY ILL by Joan K. Parry. (1989). "Should be read by all professionals engaged in the provision of health services in hospitals, emergency rooms, and hospices." *Hector B. Garcia, PhD, Professor, San Jose State University School of Social Work*

THE CREATIVE PRACTITIONER: THEORY AND METHODS FOR THE HELPING SERVICES by Bernard Gelfand. (1988). "[Should] be widely adopted by those in the helping services. It could lead to significant positive advances by countless individuals." *Sidney J. Parnes, Trustee Chairperson for Strategic Program Development, Creative Education Foundation, Buffalo, NY*

MANAGEMENT AND INFORMATION SYSTEMS IN HUMAN SERVICES: IMPLICATIONS FOR THE DISTRIBUTION OF AUTHORITY AND DECISION MAKING by Richard K. Caputo. (1987). "A contribution to social work scholarship in that it provides conceptual frameworks that can be used in the design of management information systems." *Social Work*

Order Your Own Copy of
This Important Book for Your Personal Library!

TEENAGE RUNAWAYS
Broken Hearts and "Bad Attitudes"

_____in hardbound at $29.95 (ISBN: 0-7890-0550-6)

_____in softbound at $17.95 (ISBN: 0-7890-0892-0)

COST OF BOOKS_____

OUTSIDE USA/CANADA/
MEXICO: ADD 20%_____

POSTAGE & HANDLING_____
(US: $3.00 for first book & $1.25
for each additional book)
Outside US: $4.75 for first book
& $1.75 for each additional book)

SUBTOTAL_____

IN CANADA: ADD 7% GST_____

STATE TAX_____
(NY, OH & MN residents, please
add appropriate local sales tax)

FINAL TOTAL_____
(If paying in Canadian funds,
convert using the current
exchange rate. UNESCO
coupons welcome.)

☐ **BILL ME LATER:** ($5 service charge will be added)
(Bill-me option is good on US/Canada/Mexico orders only;
not good to jobbers, wholesalers, or subscription agencies.)

☐ Check here if billing address is different from
shipping address and attach purchase order and
billing address information.

Signature_____

☐ **PAYMENT ENCLOSED: $**_____

☐ **PLEASE CHARGE TO MY CREDIT CARD.**

☐ Visa   ☐ MasterCard   ☐ AmEx   ☐ Discover
☐ Diner's Club

Account #_____

Exp. Date_____

Signature_____

Prices in US dollars and subject to change without notice.

NAME _____

INSTITUTION _____

ADDRESS _____

CITY _____

STATE/ZIP _____

COUNTRY _____ COUNTY (NY residents only) _____

TEL _____ FAX _____

E-MAIL_____

May we use your e-mail address for confirmations and other types of information? ☐ Yes   ☐ No

Order From Your Local Bookstore or Directly From
The Haworth Press, Inc.
10 Alice Street, Binghamton, New York 13904-1580 • USA
TELEPHONE: 1-800-HAWORTH (1-800-429-6784) / Outside US/Canada: (607) 722-5857
FAX: 1-800-895-0582 / Outside US/Canada: (607) 772-6362
E-mail: getinfo@haworthpressinc.com
PLEASE PHOTOCOPY THIS FORM FOR YOUR PERSONAL USE.

BOF96